THERE'S GOT TO BE MORE TO LIFE THAN THIS

Where Do You Stand?

Lawrence Eimers

*I would like to dedicate this book to Carol Camp,
who led me to Christ, as well as Stephanie
Eimers, who also modeled the love of Christ
to me. Thank you both so very much for all
your precious help, and for pointing me to the
foot of the Cross! I would also like to thank
the body of Christ at large, who have poured
into my life over the years. Praise God for His
amazing Grace and Mercies! Glory to Your Holy
and precious name, dear Lord! Thank you for
the deliverance from the bondage of sin.*

Contents

Introduction

By the grace of God, I survived a one percent chance to live when I was injured in a motorcycle accident in July of 1988—just three weeks after I married my first wife, Trish.

The following describes my own personal road-to-Damascus experience. As you may know, the Apostle Paul's plans were abruptly changed when God intervened and redirected his life. You never know what God has in mind when something happens to alter your life. But like Paul discovered, when it happens to you, it's a good idea to reassess the way you're living your life, and who you are living it for.

Initially, I spent ten and a half months in the hospital, and I was in and out of ICU four different times. I had eight different doctors racing to keep me alive. First, my right lung collapsed, and I got bilateral pneumonia. They put a trach in and hooked me up to a ventilator. My weight dropped from one hundred and sixty pounds to eighty-eight pounds, and I was put on a feeding tube. At the same time, I developed two pressure sores. One on my tailbone, and one on my shoulder due to my halo jacket. Over the years I have had six different pressure sores, four that tunneled all the way to my tailbone. They had to drill four screws into my skull to stabilize my neck. I have had bronchitis or pneumonia forty-six times, and covid once. I also had a severed femur head on my left hip that culminated over time with osteopenia. The good news is that I am in excellent health today. Other than a couple of tests recently, I have not been to the hospital in the last fifteen years. Praise God!

Through these experiences, I have come face to face with the prospect of death many times. Sixteen years ago, I landed in the hospital three times in a single twelve-month period. One of these admittances was because of pneumonia; during my stay, I turned blue three times and was put back on life support for the first time since the beginning of my injury. During this same time, I lost a large amount of my eyesight from a breathing medicine I was taking that blew past my mask into my eyes. Six months would pass before I would get most of my sight back. I was hospitalized again with bronchitis, and then a third time with an ileus when my digestive tract shut down. My doctor said he thought I was done. Sometimes, when it rains, it pours. And sometimes when it pours, it keeps pouring!

I became so exhausted, I was quietly asking God, "Please bring me home, dear Lord." I didn't see how I could go on. I was worn out from battling one thing after another that I didn't want to go on anymore. Don't misunderstand me—I love life. I just didn't think I had the strength to continue. I was correct. I didn't have the strength in myself. That's where Christ comes in.

Well, to my delight, I lived. Praise God! What I thought I wanted at a moment of exhaustion was to quit and give up. But God was bringing me to a place where I was ready to fully surrender my fleshly desires and conform fully and completely to His will. When we come to realize all our efforts have amounted to nothing in light of all eternity and are now starting to see it for what it really is and are ready to exchange it all for God's best for your life, now you have true hope and joy!

> [10] "Behold, I have refined you, but not as silver;
> I have tested you in the furnace of affliction (Isaiah 48:10 New American Standard Bible 1995).

As I have said many times over the years, my accident is the best thing that has ever happened to me. It put me flat on my back and got my undivided attention, and because of my long-term paralysis, it has kept my focus on the bigger picture. From there, a personal relationship with God Almighty was born, and I have been very blessed ever since.

> [1] The Lord is my shepherd,

I shall not want.

2 He makes me lie down in green pastures;
He leads me beside quiet waters.

3 He restores my soul;
He guides me in the paths of righteousness
For His name's sake.

4 Even though I walk through the valley of the shadow of death,
I fear no evil, for You are with me;
Your rod and Your staff, they comfort me.

5 You prepare a table before me in the presence of my enemies;
You have anointed my head with oil;
My cup overflows.

6 Surely goodness and lovingkindness will follow me all the days of my life,
And I will dwell in the house of the Lord forever (Psalm 23:1–6 New American Standard Bible 1995).

CHAPTER ONE: ARE YOU IN DENIAL?

We can all relate to the ups and downs in life that eventually cause us to search for meaning beyond simply working, eating, drinking, and having fun. In fact, if you've lived long enough, you've probably come to realize that even good days are only held together by a thin veneer of confidence.

After you've long been retired and your best years are behind you, what will it all have been for? As children, we eventually start to realize that the world we live in is no longer perfect. And when we're being honest with ourselves, we all have to admit that we're not perfect either. This uncertainty can send us in many different directions as we attempt to make sense of our lives.

Admittedly, there are countless problems in the world that we have no real answers for outside of rationalizing our sinful condition. And unless we bury these thoughts and feelings in an effort to avoid reality, we are forced to admit our complete dependence on God Almighty.

This is the part of the story that most people

don't really like to hear or talk about, and there's a good reason for that. Somehow, we feel better served by not facing the reality of our dilemma.

God reveals the answer for us in the Gospel of John.

> [19] This is the judgment, that the Light has come into the world, and men loved the darkness rather than the Light, for their deeds were evil. [20] For everyone who does evil hates the Light, and does not come to the Light for fear that his deeds will be exposed (John 3:19–20 New American Standard Bible 1995).

Think about that for a minute. We reject God because He demands us to be Holy, Righteous, and Pure. You see, along with Satan, our sin is our greatest enemy. This is what causes us to think we can hide ourselves from God. When living in denial becomes a way of life, it's not only personally destructive. Infinitely greater is the person who purposefully ignores God's forewarnings and foolishly turns his or her heart away from the truth.

> [2] But there is nothing covered up that will not be revealed, and hidden that will not be known. [3] Accordingly,

whatever you have said in the dark will be heard in the light, and what you have whispered in the inner rooms will be proclaimed upon the housetops.

[4] "I say to you, My friends, do not be afraid of those who kill the body and after that have no more that they can do. [5] But I will warn you whom to fear: fear the One who, after He has killed, has authority to cast into hell; yes, I tell you, fear Him! (Luke 12:2–5 New American Standard Bible 1995).

[22] "How long, O naive ones, will you love being simple-minded?
And scoffers delight themselves in scoffing
And fools hate knowledge?

[23]"Turn to my reproof,
Behold, I will pour out my spirit on you;
I will make my words known to you.

[24] "Because I called and you refused,
I stretched out my hand and no one paid attention;

[25] And you neglected all my counsel
And did not want my reproof;

[26] I will also laugh at your calamity;
I will mock when your dread comes,

²⁷ When your dread comes like a storm
And your calamity comes like a
whirlwind,
When distress and anguish come upon
you.

²⁸ "Then they will call on me, but I will
not answer;
They will seek me diligently but they
will not find me,

²⁹ Because they hated knowledge
And did not choose the fear of the Lord.

³⁰ "They would not accept my counsel,
They spurned all my reproof.

³¹ "So they shall eat of the fruit of their
own way
And be satiated with their own devices.

³² "For the waywardness of the naive
will kill them,
And the complacency of fools will
destroy them (Proverbs 1:22–30 New
American Standard Bible 1995).

Be very careful of the different influences in your
life. Bad ones can get you off track in a hurry and
carry you far away from the truth. Ultimately,
it could lead to your destruction. Beware of
idolatry, which is the worship of idols or excessive
devotion to a certain person or thing. An idol is

anything that attempts to replace the one true God. Idols are no more than impotent blocks of stone or wood, and their power exists only in the minds of their worshippers. Beware, idolatry goes beyond the worship of idols, images, and false gods. It can also be a matter of a person's prideful heart and self-centeredness. God is trying to do us all a favor by warning us. Secondly, be very careful concerning blasphemy. Blasphemy is to speak with contempt about God or to be defiantly irreverent toward Him. Do not express reproach toward God's Name, Character, Work, or Power. We as the body of Christ should never misrepresent the Glory, Authority, and Character of God Almighty.

I used to think I was in control of my life. That lasted until it was demonstrated to me that I was here only because God willed it to be. This understanding should be very humbling to us all, and it ought to destroy our silly human pride; but instead, we often remain resistant to the one truth that could save us.

To put this into greater perspective, none of us willed ourselves to be born into this world. It happened without our wish or consent, and yet we've been given the incredible gift of life. The truth is you can no more prevent yourself from dying than you could have brought yourself here to begin with.

So, I ask you, do you really believe that you

are the one in control? I never fully considered these things until I was forced to. It all changed for me when I was staring death right in the eye. Needless to say, such an experience gets your undivided attention.

When I first awoke in ICU about thirty days after my accident, not realizing I had been in a horrible crash that would ultimately change my life forever, my first thought was one of gratitude. I was alive, after all. I was told that I had been in an accident, that I had broken my neck, and that I would never walk again. When you are literally clinging to life, it sends you into a whole new state of mind. Everything is completely out of your control. You have very little say, other than, "Pull the plug." But then what?

One man that arrived right next door to me, had just rolled his bulldozer over on top of himself. He died two days later. Then when I arrived in rehab for the first time, I heard of another man who came into the ICU unit who had fallen off some scaffolding while working on his home. Sadly, he landed on his head, and all he could move was his eyeballs. Turns out, he was drinking and lost his balance.

As a former alcoholic, when I attempt to list the benefits of drinking alcohol, I can't come up with one. However, when you think of all the destructive ways it affects our lives, you can easily come up with a long list that should cause a person to question why would I spend my life doing so. What a total waste of time and resources.

When you think about it, there are few things that are worse than being dead. Surviving a one percent chance to live is nothing short of a miracle. It's one thing to read it in a book or see it portrayed in a movie, but to experience it in real life is a huge wake-up call.

The truth is that we as human beings take a lot for granted in life without fully considering the eternal ramifications. Sure, we might think about getting older someday, but do we truly consider the magnitude of the very moment following our departure as we pass from here into eternity?

It's alarming when I think of how easily I could have died as a result of my accident. I was not a born-again Christian at the time. That means, based on God's Holy Word, I would not have gone to Heaven had I passed away. Honestly, is there a single more important issue than that in all of life? Compare that to any other concerns that you've ever had.

One of the many things I've learned the hard way is that it's always time to urgently reflect on life and death because it could happen to any one of us at any moment. You've heard the old saying: "Here today and gone tomorrow." Trust me when I say there is it far better life that awaits us when we place our faith and trust in Jesus Christ alone for our Salvation.

The truth is we all need to purposefully examine our hearts and reflect deeply on our true condition. Unlike the person who rejected their doctor's advice and paid a heavy price, we would all be wise to heed God's warnings and observe His only way of redemption.

So, I encourage you to search your heart today as you continue to read. *Look far past what's comfortable and examine reality before God.* And don't make the mistake of comparing yourself with anyone besides Jesus Christ—Who is alone without sin. And that of course is why He alone could pay the penalty for man's sins.

> [15] For we do not have a high priest who cannot sympathize with our weaknesses, but One who has been tempted in all things as we are, yet without sin (Hebrews 4:15 New American Standard Bible 1995).

True introspection only happens when we take seriously our plight as mere human beings in rebellion against a Holy and Just God. Because of this blatant denial that we have all practiced, it often takes a life-altering situation for us to come to terms with our humanity. This serves to snap us out of our denial and causes us to consider more deeply where we truly stand with God.

It is only when you and I acknowledge the reality of our eventual death and coming judgement that we take seriously all the deceptions in this world meant to cause fear and confusion. Fear makes us think, say, and do stupid things. Of course, these distractions result in a life mostly spent on things with little to no lasting value. All by Satan's design.

The one thing that is as undeniable as it is universal is that we have all sinned and fall short of the Glory of God. The truth is, if your hope of spending eternity in Heaven doesn't include the redemption of your sin based on the one sacrifice acceptable to God, then you are gravely mistaken, and will be separated from the love and presence of the One True God forever.

A time is coming when it will be too late. You will either be under the blood of Jesus Christ, or you will stand there on judgment day wishing you would have lived an entirely different life!

> [5] But if any of you lacks wisdom, let him ask of God, who gives to all generously and without reproach, and it will be given to him. [6] But he must ask in faith without any doubting, for the one who doubts is like the surf of the sea, driven and tossed by the wind. [7] For that

man ought not to expect that he will receive anything from the Lord, [8] being a double-minded man, unstable in all his ways (James 1:5–8 New American Standard Bible 1995).

As you consider your future, remember that there is only One individual who ever died for your sins, and lived to talk about it, and that is the Lord Jesus Christ. Because of this, He will judge our lives in a Holy and Righteous manner and riding the fence will not be an option. Now, someone might say, but how can God send someone to hell if they have never heard the Gospel? Good question. Let's see what God's Word says about that:

[18] For the wrath of God is revealed from heaven against all ungodliness and unrighteousness of men who suppress the truth in unrighteousness, [19] because that which is known about God is evident within them; for God made it evident to them. [20] For since the creation of the world His invisible attributes, His eternal power and divine nature, have been clearly seen, being understood through what has been made, so that they are without

excuse (Romans 1:18–20 New American Standard Bible 1995).

Is not the earth and the entire universe filled with His Glory? And even if a person was blind, our conscience bears witness to the truth so that we are without excuse.

So, it is not that some people have not heard the Gospel, but rather that they have rejected what they have heard. Of course, this is not God in a vague sense, this is the God of the Bible —the Godhead of Father, Son (Jesus), and the Holy Spirit. This innate understanding confers responsibility on all humans. God is not to be trifled with, as the passage goes on to clarify:

> [21] For even though they knew God, they did not honor Him as God or give thanks, but they became futile in their speculations, and their foolish heart was darkened. [22] Professing to be wise, they became fools, [23] and exchanged the glory of the incorruptible God for an image in the form of corruptible man and of birds and four-footed animals and crawling creatures.
>
> [24] Therefore God gave them over in the lusts of their hearts to impurity, so that their bodies would be dishonored

among them. [25] For they exchanged the truth of God for a lie, and worshiped and served the creature rather than the Creator, who is blessed forever. Amen.

[26] For this reason God gave them over to degrading passions; for their women exchanged the natural function for that which is unnatural, [27] and in the same way also the men abandoned the natural function of the woman and burned in their desire toward one another, men with men committing indecent acts and receiving in their own persons the due penalty of their error (Romans 1:21–27 New American Standard Bible 1995).

As we see here, the proliferation of sin is not isolated. Sin leads to more sin, so much so that God eventually washes his hands of the sinner. He is gracious, yes, and He is merciful, of course—but He is *Just*, too. This is a terrifying prospect to those who have turned their back on God.

A lot of people say hell isn't real because they are in denial, and they have bought into their own rationalism. Repentance to the One True God is our only hope. Humble yourself today and get right with the Lord before it's too late!

Following my spinal cord injury, I went

through some of the toughest seasons of my life—seasons that drove me to the end of self-many times over. Eventually, my pride and selfish desires died out under the weight of total hopelessness and helplessness, which was the best thing that could have ever happened to me!

When it comes to pride, there are two sides to the coin. One is the feeling you get when you do a good job at work or when a family member or friend accomplishes something. But God hates pride that comes from self-righteousness or arrogance. The latter leads to sin and hinders us from humbly seeking Him, which is in our very best interest.

> [3] "Blessed are the poor in spirit, for theirs is the kingdom of heaven (Matthew 5:3 New American Standard Bible 1995).

True humility is when a person recognizes their utter inability to come to God aside from His Divine Grace. The proud, however, are so blinded by their pride that they think they have no need for God, or they think that they're good enough on their own merits; so much so that God will accept them into heaven just as they are.

> [18] For it is not he who commends himself that is approved, but he whom the

Lord commends (2 Corinthians 10:18 New American Standard Bible 1995).

Pride becomes sinful when we give ourselves credit for something that God has done. Pride is taking the glory that belongs to God and keeping it for ourselves, as if the Fall of Mankind never happened. We are essentially worshipping self. In doing so, we become our own god—a notion which lands a person in hell forever.

> [7] For who regards you as superior? What do you have that you did not receive? And if you did receive it, why do you boast as if you had not received it? (1 Corinthians 4:7 New American Standard Bible 1995).

Humility in the Bible is described as meekness and lowliness—in other words, an absence of self. Think of dying to self, which is a necessity to become Christlike. Humility is a heart attitude, not just an outward demeanor. A person can act humble on the outside, but on the inside be full of pride and self-importance. God is not fooled.

> [46] These will go away into eternal punishment, but the righteous into eternal life." (Matthew 25:46 New American Standard Bible 1995).

^{36} He who believes in the Son has eternal life; but he who does not obey the Son will not see life, but the wrath of God abides on him." (John 3:36 New American Standard Bible 1995).

I came to realize that a correct perspective is a dependable roadmap, and that it is worth whatever we go through to get it.

> ^{23} Thus says the Lord, "Let not a wise man boast of his wisdom, and let not the mighty man boast of his might, let
>
> not a rich man boast of his riches; ^{24} but let him who boasts boast of this, that he understands and knows Me, that I am the Lord who exercises lovingkindness, justice and righteousness on earth; for I delight in these things," declares the Lord (Jeremiah 9:23–24 New American Standard Bible 1995).

Have you ever wondered why we go through one trial after another? One reason is that we quickly forget. We can believe something one minute and be good with it, and then minutes later, we're right back where we were, complaining about our circumstances.

It's only when we learn to persevere

through various difficulties that we begin to learn important lessons that lead to meaningful outcomes. The valuable lessons learned from challenging experiences like these far exceed the superficial feelings that quickly crumple when challenged by even the least of things in life. Instead of seeing trials as something negative, we should view each of them as an opportunity to grow in the moment. This cannot be accomplished if a person is still living in their sinful nature as a result of the Fall of mankind.

Whether a person likes to admit it at first or not, only Christ has done, and only He can do what is needed most, and that is to save your very soul from eternal damnation. He gives you a new nature. One that desires and longs to praise, worship, serve, honor, and thank God for His amazing Grace, Mercies, Love, and Power. For all that and much more, we should be extremely grateful, should we not?

We are just a tiny little speck in the universe, and this knowledge alone should humble us to the point where we begin to ponder where we came from. Do you honestly believe we evolved from monkeys? This is another one of Satan's schemes. Because of our sinful nature we cling to this nonsense to help us sleep at night to try to justify the sin in our lives somehow. God didn't kick Adam and Eve out of the Garden of Eden for nothing.

As human beings, we are designed with an unmatched opportunity to experience life in a way that only we can. As we engage in this incredible endeavor, our lives take on many different turns, and with each new experience, it teaches us something new about ourselves in relation to God's unique plan for our lives.

Five years following my accident, I learned again just how precious the gift of life is when I lost my mom. She was dropping some items off at my brother- and sister-in-law's home for her grandchildren. Traveling a short distance on a blustery winter morning, she was struck and killed instantly by a train as she crossed the tracks. She was only forty-nine years old.

It's hard to put into words what it's like to experience such a tragedy. There is absolutely no good answer for this outside of the biblical account that describes the fall of mankind, and the subsequent curses that befell humanity.

Life is unique to us all in the way that we come in and out of this world. Sometimes we're given a heads up when we're told we have six months to live, and other times our lives can come to an end in a split second. Many people go to bed at night and simply don't wake up in the morning.

One thing is for sure, and that is we will all experience the ultimate event of passing from here into eternity, where life will never end. This journey will be the result of the many decisions that *we ourselves have made*, and how we've responded to the call of God on our lives.

For some, Heaven will be an incredible culmination of a believer's life spent knowing, growing, and serving God. But for others, God's momentary presence at judgment day will only be a memory of a time when repentance was possible during the age of grace that has now come to an end.

CHAPTER TWO:
COMING TO TERMS
WITH REALITY

There are countless stories that could be told that would greatly impact your life. But there is only one that will really matter in the end. And that is where you stood with Jesus Christ.

I would consider myself a failure before my injury. All I did was work, party, and raise Cain. The good news is it didn't end there. Without much more than a high school education, my life started over. It was as though someone had hit the reset button, and I was given a second chance. Only this time, I would have to attempt it without the use of my legs, and only partial use of my arms and hands.

This doesn't exactly describe a warrior who's preparing for battle, but that's exactly where I found myself. I was in a fight for my very existence. It was through this experience that I began to realize just how deeply precious life really is. Every single one of our lives is unique—something we should never take for granted.

Although this book is a true story about how I survived nearly impossible odds, it's really more about you, the reader. You see, God uses the trials in our lives to shape and mold us on our journey back into His Kingdom through faith in His Son, Jesus Christ. As Paul's epistle to the Romans says:

> [28] And we know that God causes all things to work together for good to those who love God, to those who are called according to His purpose. [29] For those whom He foreknew, He also predestined to become conformed to the image of His Son, so that He would be the firstborn among many brethren; [30] and these whom He predestined, He also called; and these whom He called, He also justified; and these whom He justified, He also glorified. [31] What then shall we say to these things? If God is for us, who is against us? (Romans 8:28–31 New American Standard Bible 1995).

No matter what your situation may be today, and no matter what your past may remind you of, there's always hope for you right where you're at. As I lay there on that unforgettable day, unable to move my legs or even sit up, I knew something had gone terribly wrong. I had always been used to walking away. What I thought was going to be the real battle—which was spending the rest of my life paralyzed—was only a steppingstone to the next chapter of my life.

There are a lot of things in life—like divorce, poverty, famine, and war—that make our lives much more difficult. But the greater battle that we face is far less understood. This particular war that I speak of is being waged from deep within each of us, as well as all around us. Until you understand what is truly happening and accept the reality of your circumstances in relation to God, you will remain powerless. You will go on fighting the same old battles, year after year, decade after decade.

I urge you to think very carefully about this. There is no Plan B. Life was created by God, and this is His only arrangement for our Salvation. Now we can agree to disagree about some things in life, but to throw Christ and the Bible out with the bathwater and still expect to be cleansed by the blood of the Lamb is completely reckless.

In the second chapter of Ephesians, we read of someone who formally lived without God, and the result of this common way of life:

> [1] And you were dead in your trespasses and sins, [2] in which you formerly

walked according to the course of this world, according to the prince of the power of the air, of the spirit that is now

working in the sons of disobedience. [3] Among them we too all formerly lived in the lusts of our flesh, indulging the desires of the flesh and of the mind, and were by nature children of wrath, even as the rest (Ephesians 2:1–3 New American Standard Bible 1995).

These three verses don't exactly paint a pretty picture of what we're often like, but it does state the truth of what we all experience from one degree to another. So, whether you are aware of it or not, you're fighting an enemy—Satan—who is trying to destroy you and everything that is good in the world. The first battlefield in this war takes place in our minds, and (if you allow Satan to control your thinking) he will control your life which will not end well.

[4] in whose case the god of this world has blinded the minds of the unbelieving so that they might not see the light of the gospel of the glory of Christ, who is the image of God (2 Corinthians 4:4 New American Standard Bible 1995).

Always remember, Satan does everything he can

to try to undermine God's Word. His goal is to destroy God's people and discredit the cause of Christ. Satan intentionally tries to forget what Jesus said on the Cross. The Lord's words, "It is finished," meant that He had just defeated Satan, death, hell, and the grave. The devil's remaining time on this earth is numbered. Praise our Lord and Savior Jesus Christ!

> [1] Now I make known to you, brethren, the gospel which I preached to you, which also you received, in which also you stand, [2] by which also you are saved, if you hold fast the word which I preached to you, unless you believed in vain.
>
> [3] For I delivered to you as of first importance what I also received, that Christ died for our sins according to the Scriptures, [4] and that He was buried, and that He was raised on the third day according to the Scriptures, [5] and that He appeared to Cephas, then to the twelve. [6] After that He appeared to more than five hundred brethren at one time, most of whom remain until now, but some have fallen asleep; [7] then He appeared to James, then to all the

apostles; [8] and last of all, as to one untimely born, He appeared to me also. [9] For I am the least of the apostles, and not fit to be called an apostle, because I persecuted the church of God. [10] But by the grace of God I am what I am, and His grace toward me did not prove vain; but I labored even more than all of them, yet not I, but the grace of God with me. [11] Whether then it was I or they, so we preach and so you believed.

[12] Now if Christ is preached, that He has been raised from the dead, how do some among you say that there is no resurrection of the dead? [13] But if there is no resurrection of the dead, not even Christ has been raised; [14] and if Christ has not been raised, then our preaching is vain, your faith also is vain. [15] Moreover we are even found to be false witnesses of God, because we testified against God that He raised Christ, whom He did not raise, if in fact the dead are not raised. [16] For if the dead are not raised, not even Christ has been raised; [17] and if Christ has not

been raised, your faith is worthless; you are still in your sins. [18] Then those also who have fallen asleep in Christ have perished. [19] If we have hoped in Christ in this life only, we are of all men most to be pitied.

[20] But now Christ has been raised from the dead, the first fruits of those who are asleep. [21] For since by a man came death, by a man also came the resurrection of the dead. [22] For as in Adam all die, so also in Christ all will be made alive. [23] But each in his own order: Christ the first fruits, after that those who are Christ's at His coming, [24] then comes the end, when He hands over the kingdom to the God and Father, when He has abolished all rule and all authority and power. [25] For He must reign until He has put all His enemies under His feet. [26] The last enemy that will be abolished is death. [27] For He has put all things in subjection under His feet. But when He says, "All things are put in subjection," it is evident that He is excepted who put

all things in subjection to Him. [28] When all things are subjected to Him, then the Son Himself also will be subjected to the One who subjected all things to Him, so that God may be all in all (1 Corinthians 15:1–28 New American Standard Bible 1995).

You cannot earn forgiveness from God. You cannot pay for the forgiveness of your sins. You can only receive it through faith in Christ's Death and Resurrection.

In order to truly begin to change your life, you're going to have to come to a place where you are sincerely repentant of your sin and ask God for forgiveness. This usually doesn't happen until we have completely run out of options and we're willing to listen to what He's been trying to tell us all along.

To this end, terrible tragedies and a countless number of other challenges in life can be turned into valuable opportunities that can benefit us greatly if we respond in faith. It can change the way you see God, and a personal relationship with God Himself can follow the moment you believe. So, when you look at your current circumstances—no matter what that may involve—don't ever underestimate Christ's death and Resurrection from the grave. This guarantees all who believe victory over every situation, and every enemy that we will ever face in this life, no matter who or what that may be.

If you are ready to accept Jesus Christ as your Savior and Lord, and receive forgiveness from God, it is only attainable by believing and trusting in Jesus Christ. For example, you could say a prayer like, "God, I know I have sinned against You, and deserve death. But Jesus took the punishment that I deserved so that through faith in Him, I could be forgiven of all my sins. I place all my faith and trust in You, and You alone. Thank You for Your precious grace and mercies, and for the forgiveness of my sins. Amen."

You are meant to live a life of significance. God desires to change your life, and to leave behind all the things that are not of Him. One way He does this is by using our circumstances to bring us to the end of hope in ourselves. See it as an act of His grace and mercies. Only then can we begin to refocus our time and attention on Him and His Eternal Kingdom.

The plans that God has for your life and mine are the target of Satan, who deceives us into believing his lies. Instead of seeing the trials in our lives as opportunities, we tend to blame God for our problems. And instead of redirecting our lives back toward God, we often remain focused on things that bring us instant gratification rather than trusting in God's eternal rewards.

¹⁰ For we must all appear before the judgment seat of Christ, so that each one may be recompensed for his deeds in the body, according to what he has done, whether good or bad (2 Corinthians 5:10 New American Standard Bible 1995).

If you want to experience true peace in your life, then learn to win the war. You must take every thought captive to the obedience of Christ and avoid being controlled by the different strongholds that Satan sets up in our minds as children. This is immensely important.

You see, prior to my Salvation in Christ, I never realized my sinful condition and the consequences of this in relation to a Holy God. But now that I have the revelation of Jesus Christ, I can see this sinful, fallen, cursed world for what it is, and the results of my sinful lifestyle that had followed me my whole life.

The good news is that a year and a half into my injury, when I was twenty-six years old, I prayed a simple prayer of faith and was set free from the bondage of my sinful nature that controlled how I thought and behaved.

For example, I started drinking at the age of nine. I became an alcoholic by the time I reached high school in an effort to numb the pain of rejection and abandonment. Although I didn't understand it at the time, it doesn't make it any less real. I smoked cigarettes, I did drugs. I looked at pornography. I slept with girls and took something from them that did not belong to me. Shame on me!

It doesn't matter how young you are, it's still fornication in God's eyes, and that's sin. This is a conversation parents need to have with their children at the right time. I did it again when I met Trish. Moreover, I lied and stole. I could go on and on. This isn't uncommon. Sadly, this is our sinful nature in action, and we all must repent and seek God's forgiveness.

> [9] Or do you not know that the unrighteous will not inherit the kingdom of God? Do not be deceived; neither fornicators, nor idolaters, nor adulterers, nor effeminate, nor homosexuals, [10] nor thieves, nor the covetous, nor drunkards, nor revilers, nor swindlers, will inherit the kingdom of God. [11] Such were some of you; but you were washed, but you were sanctified, but you were justified in the name of the Lord Jesus Christ and in the Spirit of our God (1 Corinthians 6:9-11 New American Standard Bible 1995).

¹⁹ Or do you not know that your body is a temple of the Holy Spirit who is in you, whom you have from God, and that you are not your own? ²⁰ For you have been bought with a price: therefore glorify God in your body (1 Corinthians 6:19-20 New American Standard Bible 1995).

In spite of all that wicked sin, by the grace of God, He forgave me when I asked for His forgiveness, and I was given a new nature and filled with the Holy Spirit. This gives me the power to live victoriously every day. I was given a fresh new start in life that now included my Lord and Savior, Jesus Christ. Along with that, I received a whole new purpose that God Himself designed for me personally. You see, it was by God's grace alone and nothing else that granted me life when I was facing a one percent chance to live. God Himself reached down from Heaven and intervened, and He wants to do the same in your life today. This proves no matter how difficult your situation may appear, there is always hope! When you and I encounter trials like these, we quickly learn just how dependent we really are on God.

I urge you today. Humble yourself before the Cross. Get down on your knees and ask God for the forgiveness of your sins by placing your faith in Christ's death and Resurrection alone.

The word "forgive" means to pardon someone for something they did. To cancel a debt. It is a voluntary expression of love, grace, and mercy toward others. The greatest example of this is when Jesus Christ died on the Cross for our sins.

The question is, do you want to have your sins forgiven by God?

[7] In Him we have redemption through His blood, the forgiveness of our trespasses, according to the riches of His grace (Ephesians 1:7 New American Standard Bible 1995).

[2] and He Himself is the propitiation for our sins; and not for ours only, but also for those of the whole world (1 John 2:2 New American Standard Bible 1995).

[8] If we say that we have no sin, we are deceiving ourselves and the truth is not in us (1 John 1:8 New American Standard Bible 1995).

No matter what you have done. No matter what you are going through. No matter how impossible life may seem at the moment, you must believe that God has the power to do a miracle in your life. Believe that He will turn your entire world around just like He did mine. This extends to the way you interact with Him as well as how you see your place and purpose in the world today. It's based on a personal intimate relationship with a Holy and Sovereign God. Remember, we will spend all eternity either with Him in Heaven, or without Him in hell.

I don't fear death. I can't wait to pass over into eternity, and it's not because I'm crippled. It's because I can't wait to see my Lord in all His Splendor and Glory, and all of Heaven that He created for His blessed children. And with a brand-new set of lungs and a glorified body, I will enthusiastically praise my Lord and Savior alongside my precious wife Michelle and all our brothers and sisters in Christ forever and ever. Amen!

Even though I might be considered by some today as half a man, that doesn't remotely describe how I feel or believe. If God can take my life and turn it around as He has, He can do it for you or anyone else who believes.

> [21] For to me, to live is Christ and to die is gain. [22] But if I am to live on in the flesh, this will mean fruitful labor for me; and I do not know which to choose. [23] But

I am hard-pressed from both directions, having the desire to depart and be with Christ, for that is very much better; [24] yet to remain on in the flesh is more necessary for your sake (Philippians 1:21–24 New American Standard Bible 1995).

In your personal search for meaning and purpose over the last ten to twenty years, have you truly discovered what is most important in life? Have you really thought your way through all the advertisements and got to the real deal?

[3] For the time already past is sufficient for you to have carried out the desire of the Gentiles, having pursued a course of sensuality, lusts, drunkenness, carousing, drinking parties and abominable idolatries. [4] In all this, they are surprised that you do not run with them into the same excesses of dissipation, and they malign you; [5] but they will give account to Him who is ready to judge the living and the dead (1 Peter 4:3–5 New American Standard Bible 1995).

If I were you, I would pause right here and

think this through. God doesn't wait until we're dead to judge us; it begins here in this life. What explanation will you give to Him that will be consistent with Scripture concerning your Salvation? Will you explain that you were a good person compared to some others that you knew? Will you try to give some examples of good works that you've done to add to Christ's death on the Cross, as if that were possible?

One of the hardest things to do is to listen to news that we don't want to hear. That's why we often stay away from doctor's offices, not to mention a Bible-based church. But whether you're trying to avoid your doctor or a pastor, it's never a good idea to avoid the truth. Whatever has the potential to be difficult in life does not improve by ignoring it. As described in 2 Timothy, it doesn't work that way:

> [1] I solemnly charge you in the presence of God and of Christ Jesus, who is to judge the living and the dead, and by His appearing and His kingdom: [2] preach the word; be ready in season and out of season; reprove, rebuke, exhort, with great patience and instruction. [3] For the time will come when they will not endure sound doctrine; but wanting to have their ears tickled, they will

accumulate for themselves teachers in accordance to their own desires, [4] and will turn away their ears from the truth and will turn aside to myths. [5] But you, be sober in all things, endure hardship, do the work of an evangelist, fulfill your ministry (2 Timothy 4:1–5 New American Standard Bible 1995).

With all this in mind, let's have a candid conversation. Please know I do not say this with any judgment toward anyone. I say this with deep-hearted concern. Take a look at the following verse:

[27] And inasmuch as it is appointed for men to die once and after this comes judgment (Hebrews 9:27 New American Standard Bible 1995).

This should be at the forefront of everyone's mind. We urgently need to open our eyes and cry out to God Almighty for His forgiveness before it's too late! The night before my mom's accident she updated her to-do list. She gathered the items she had prepared to drop off the next day. She jumped out of bed in the morning like everyone else. She planned to be back home before long. Guess what: it didn't happen. Unexpected deaths happen every day. If we are not careful, we will miss God's perfectly intended purpose for our lives. Live life today; yesterday is gone, and tomorrow may never come.

Once our opportunity has passed, there's no second chance—there's no turning back. Our short-sighted focus is at best the next few years, rather than taking a complete view of eternity.

Understanding the temporal nature of this life helps us to live proactively. You will understand things almost as if in hindsight because you will be looking at it from an eternal perspective rather than just day to day.

Instead of measuring the value of your life by the car you drive, the home you live in, or how much money you have in the bank, you should be measuring the capacity of your heart toward the things of God.

> [12] For the word of God is living and active and sharper than any two-edged sword, and piercing as far as the division of soul and spirit, of both joints and marrow, and able to judge the thoughts and intentions of the heart (Hebrews 4:12 New American Standard Bible 1995).

Unfortunately, many people today have lost sight of this standard. They have traded it in for a counterfeit lifestyle that tries to replace God for an unrealistic dream that will end at God's front door. I fear many will realize this too late; that God's plan for their life was perfect, but they never gave Him the time of day.

CHAPTER THREE: CHANGING PATHS

If you've lived long enough, you know that change can be difficult. I'm not talking about changing jobs or the kind of cereal you eat. I'm talking about redefining your whole life—*relationships included*. Change of this scale begins in your heart and mind. How many times have you faced the need to drastically change something in your life only to find yourself fighting hard against it at first?

We don't generally make the kind of changes we know we need to make unless there are lingering problems associated with them. This tends to force us to take the kind of action we know we need to, but we lack the understanding, courage, discipline, or desire to do it on our own. Ask yourself a question. Am I the same person I was a year ago, six months ago, or one month ago?

When you honestly consider who you are without a true, intimate relationship with God, it leaves you with little to no hope. That is why it is so important to learn to look at life differently.

As strange as it might sound at first, one of the keys to change is to begin to see the trials in your life as an actual blessing. You need to train your mind to look past the difficulties that you're going through to discover the purpose of these experiences. Think of it as a spiritual exercise to help you grow and mature as a person, a couple, and as parents.

Take the following passage, for example. Let these three verses be a measuring stick concerning your relationships and spiritual growth.

> [2] Consider it all joy, my brethren, when you encounter various trials, [3] knowing that the testing of your faith produces endurance. [4] And let endurance have its perfect result, so that you may be perfect and complete, lacking in nothing (James 1:2–4 New American Standard Bible 1995).

Pay close attention to verse 2: "Consider it all joy, my brethren, when you encounter various trials." What is your typical response when you go from one trial to the next each week? Have you gotten to the place where you are able to be at total peace, recognizing the opportunity to experience the Power of God's Word in action? Or do you think the idea of personally experiencing various trials as times of joy is a completely silly notion?

The next two verses explain God's intentions. He says, "Knowing that the testing of your faith produces endurance. And let endurance have its perfect result, so that you may be perfect and complete, lacking in nothing." When we completely focus on God's Word, and apply it immediately in faith, without acting out of our flesh, we supernaturally grow in Christlikeness! This is priceless as a Christian. Cry out to Him, "Create in me a clean heart, dear Lord."

> [11] For everyone who exalts himself will be humbled, and he who humbles himself will be exalted." (Luke 14:11 New American Standard Bible 1995).

I came across the following passage several months after experiencing complete peace in the middle of a difficult situation. It confirms the working power of the Holy Spirit in our lives as Christians.

> [1] Simon Peter, a bond-servant and apostle of Jesus Christ, to those who have received a faith of the same kind as ours, by the righteousness of our God and Savior, Jesus Christ: [2] Grace

and peace be multiplied to you in the knowledge of God and of Jesus our Lord; [3] seeing that His divine power has granted to us everything pertaining to life and godliness, through the true knowledge of Him who called us by His own glory and excellence. [4] For by these He has granted to us His precious and magnificent promises, so that by them you may become partakers of the divine nature, having escaped the corruption that is in the world by lust. [5] Now for this very reason also, applying all diligence, in your faith supply moral excellence, and in your moral excellence, knowledge, [6] and in your knowledge, self-control, and in your self-control, perseverance, and in your perseverance, godliness, [7] and in your godliness, brotherly kindness, and in your brotherly kindness, love. [8] For if these qualities are yours and are increasing, they render you neither useless nor unfruitful in the true knowledge of our Lord Jesus Christ. [9] For he who lacks these qualities is blind or short-sighted, having forgotten his purification from his former sins. [10] Therefore, brethren, be all the more diligent to make certain about His calling and choosing you; for as long as you practice these things, you will never stumble; [11] for in this way the entrance into the eternal kingdom of our Lord and Savior Jesus Christ will be abundantly supplied to you (2 Peter 1:1–11 New American Standard Bible 1995).

Is your heart weighed down because of all the troubles of this world? Naturally, unrealistic expectations or perspectives cause unnecessary fear. It's true, down here on earth troubles are never far away. It's always going to be something. But don't give in to the darkness around you. Satan wants to destroy your life. Get wise to his lies. Do not let your heart be troubled, nor let it be fearful. Tell him to go to hell where he belongs for ruining so many people's lives!

Righteous change does not come naturally to us. Only God can give you the desire and power to change fundamentally. That's why God's Word is so life changing!

When you think about the different possibilities that explain all the problems in life, the biblical account clearly describes the world as we know it. In short, it addresses the problems we face perfectly, graciously, and truthfully. So, when you think about the trials that you have gone through or are going through at the moment, it's much more than a result of unfortunate circumstances. It's really the result of a much deeper problem that goes back to a time when man decided to follow his own course in life and not God's. Because of this, it links directly back to man's pride and rebellion in the Garden of Eden against a Holy and Righteous God.

If you continue to listen to terrible advice and misdiagnose the real problem, then you will continue to live a lie. You yourself will have decided to continue to avoid God rather than come to Him for the help that we all desperately need. If your doctor misdiagnoses a medical problem that you're having and you continue to live your life under false pretenses, then there could be serious ramifications. But if you learn to trust God and His Sovereignty for your redemption, then you will have nothing to fear—not even death.

Following a spinal cord injury, some people might believe a person's life would be severely limited. But if you can learn to see beyond the temporary, then you can begin to change your outlook immediately, no matter what your situation may be. This means learning to live in such a way that positively affects not only your life, but the lives of others. Then the things that happen to you in this life take on a completely different meaning, which gives purpose beyond the temporal.

My wife Michelle and I have a great passion to share the love of Christ with others. For many years we remained stuck going around the same old mountain. Losing the same old battles. Specifically, we were being deceived by Satan and his cohorts, and being controlled by strongholds in our minds. This is not the way you want to live your life. Pray for the destruction of all strongholds in your life.

Deceptions such as these take hold during difficult times in our childhood, when our minds are still being hardwired. And they greatly affect us in our teenage and adult lives until we get wise to it and change our approach.

It wasn't until Michelle and I *strictly applied God's Word alone* that we began to experience true peace like never before.

Fear is one of Satan's favorite tools. You can see why. It's very effective if we do not have a clear understanding of God's Word and exercise our faith. There is no reason to live in fear! Now, however, there is a healthy fear:

> [25] The fear of man brings a snare,
> But he who trusts in the Lord will be exalted (Proverbs 29:25 New American Standard Bible 1995).

> [17] Honor all people, love the brotherhood, fear God, honor the king (1 Peter 2:17 New American Standard Bible 1995).

It's critical to your wellbeing that you don't let the concerns of this world overwhelm and rob you of your hope. Quiet your mind and be at peace. Why live in a state of anxiety? Learn to be very intentional in replacing all of your old ways of thinking.

> [7] For God has not given us a spirit of timidity, but of power and love and discipline (2 Timothy 1:7 New American Standard Bible 1995).

When concern becomes dread, and your feelings override God's Word, an alarm is triggered, and away you go down the same old road.

> [7] Submit therefore to God. Resist the devil and he will flee from you (James 4:7 New American Standard Bible 1995).

All our thoughts and communication must be based on God's Holy Word. This assures us that we are basing our decisions on the truth, and the truth is what sets us free from all unhealthy fear.

¹⁰⁵ Your word is a lamp to my feet and a light to my path (Psalm 119:105 New American Standard Bible 1995).

Never forget. Everything else must go. Anything that is not consistent with the Bible should no longer be a part of your life, your marriage, or you're parenting. Don't add or subtract anything to God's precious Word. We do so to our own demise. Why be oppressed by worry, fear, and anxiety for the rest of your life? How has it ever benefited anyone since the Fall of Mankind? All it does is keep a person stuck verses maturing and overcoming so you can move on to greater and greater things in life, all for God's Glory, and our good.

The biblical command "Do not fear" does not negate the daily need for foresight and caution in this world. We need to be praying for wisdom and discernment every day of our lives. Then trust and believe with all your heart.

We all need the Prince of Peace at work in our lives. The kind of peace that no one can ever take from you. As you *fully* trust God, you will be able to experience complete peace like you've never imagined. And it only gets better from there as you continue to submit to and obey God's Word. Like when you're in the middle of an argument with your spouse, for example. When they are upset about something, and you are able to experience one hundred percent peace before God Almighty—even if the argument continues for a half hour or longer. You can only find divine strength like this through a personal intimate relationship with God Himself.

> [18] If possible, so far as it depends on you, be at peace with all men (Romans 12:18 New American Standard Bible 1995).

We start out by pointing our fingers at each other. Blaming each other. Being disrespectful. Even unkind. Then we grow weary, and we start to lose hope. Exactly what Satan wants us to do!

Moving forward— Your motivation should never be out of fear, but love. While you learn to remain at total peace, it will graciously expose your spouse's different strongholds. And when the shoe is on the other foot, it will expose your own strongholds. The point is, while one spouse remains at total peace, it highlights the other spouse's lack of Christlikeness. You don't have to engage; God will speak to your spouse's heart. Your job is to remain at complete peace however long it takes. When you are in the middle of a conflict, it is very important to view all words spoken as coming from strongholds.

> [2] with all humility and gentleness,

with patience, showing tolerance for one another in love, ³ being diligent to preserve the unity of the Spirit in the bond of peace (Ephesians 4:2–3 New American Standard Bible 1995).

Notice the section in verse two, where it says, "Showing tolerance for one another in love." That indicates that our love should be unconditional. This is a must if we are to grow in Christlikeness.

Along with meditating on different Bible verses and praying, repeat the phrase "Therefore I am well content…", taken from 2 Corinthians 12:10. Notice that God says, "well content"—not just "content." Secondly, repeat the phrase, "My love for my spouse is not conditional." Say it over and over and over. Remember, transform your heart, and renew your mind. As a word of caution, if you don't remain *steadfast* from day-to-day, you will experience a clear pattern of dropping the ball and repeating the same mistakes as before. When you slip up, it helps to go through your verses and prayerfully meditate on them soon after.

² May mercy and peace and love be multiplied to you (Jude 1:2 New American Standard Bible 1995).

³³ These things I have spoken to you,

so that in Me you may have peace. In the world you have tribulation, but take courage; I have overcome the world." (John 16:33 New American Standard Bible).

To be very clear, I'm not talking about just burying your anger for the time being. Or feeling resentful inside, and fake like you're at peace. That's just pretending. I'm talking about actually being at complete peace. Hand to God Almighty as you intentionally, totally *trust and believe in God's Word alone!* Michelle and I are now joyfully anticipating our next step in growing in Christlikeness. Glory to God Almighty always and forever!

> [22] But prove yourselves doers of the word, and not merely hearers who delude themselves (James 1: 22 New American Standard Bible 1995).

This can't be overstated; we must meditate on God's Word regularly! Just like you eat and drink daily. Break it down from one word to the next. Dig deep. Be intentional. Look at a dozen different verses at a time as you gleam critical points from each one. Then apply them to your marriage relationship. Toward your parenting. Toward your neighbor. Circle key points and apply them in faith as you completely rest in God's promises. Be determined not to continue with the same old responses any longer. God will honor your faith!

This can only be done through the Power of the Holy Spirit. Once you experience it for yourself, it becomes real to you, and it is no longer just something written on paper, or someone's opinion. From there, you simply continue to repeat the process one moment at a time until it becomes the new norm. Be sensitive to the council of the Holy Spirit. Filter everything through the Word of God. This is how you truly heal, grow, and mature from the inside out, all by God's design! Then you will be able to say to yourself, "It is well with my soul; praise His name," as you experience victory over every Goliath in your life. This is known as divine tranquility.

> [3] Keeping away from strife is an honor for a man,
> But any fool will quarrel (Proverbs 20:3 New American Standard Bible 1995).

> [27] Peace I leave with you; My peace I give to you; not as the world gives do I give to you. Do not let your heart be troubled, nor let it be fearful (John 14:27 New American Standard Bible 1995).

⁹ And He has said to me, "My grace is sufficient for you, for power is perfected in weakness." Most gladly, therefore, I will rather boast about my weaknesses, so that the power of Christ may dwell in me. ¹⁰ Therefore I am well content with weaknesses, with insults, with distresses, with persecutions, with difficulties, for Christ's sake; for when I am weak, then I am strong (2 Corinthians 12:9–10 New American Standard Bible 1995).

²¹ For you have been called for this purpose, since Christ also suffered for you, leaving you an example for you to follow in His steps, ²² who committed no sin, nor was any deceit found in His mouth; ²³ and while being reviled, He did not revile in return; while suffering, He uttered no threats, but kept entrusting Himself to Him who judges righteously (1 Peter 2:21–23 New American Standard Bible 1995).

The true meaning of life is not material in nature. Rarely do we begin to realize this until we experience something so life changing that it shakes the foundation of our beliefs. One way this happens is when we come to realize our own mortality and begin to rethink the way we're living our lives. The trials in your life are what got your undivided attention. Now they can potentially change the way you live the rest of your life if you make wiser decisions moving forward.

What really limits us in life is when our view of God is not a biblical one; when our lives do not reflect God's purpose for us while we are here on earth. Without a personal relationship with God that is consistent with the teaching of Scripture, it is impossible to please Him. So, if your life doesn't reflect Christ's life in any way, then you have to question whether you really know God as your Heavenly Father. The consequence of a Christ-filled life is summed up in John 15 and Galatians 5:

> [8] My Father is glorified by this, that you bear much fruit, and so prove to be My disciples (John 15:8 New American Standard Bible 1995).

> [22] But the fruit of the Spirit is love, joy, peace, patience, kindness, goodness, faithfulness, [23] gentleness, self-control; against such things there is no

law (Galatians 5:22-23 New American Standard Bible 1995).

When our temporary problems in this life become vehicles for God's use to share hope and truth with others, then our problems have miraculously become a means for great change. It not only impacts our lives for the good, but the lives of others as well. When this happens, everything else in life becomes irrelevant compared to the opportunities to grow in our faith. In doing so, we bring glory to God, and our lives are greatly blessed, which was the whole reason we were created to begin with. As Jesus' encounter with the blind man in John 9 illustrates, God often uses tragedy to enact true change.

> [1] As He passed by, He saw a man blind from birth. [2] And His disciples asked Him, "Rabbi, who sinned, this man or his parents, that he would be born blind?" [3] Jesus answered, "It was neither that this man sinned, nor his parents; but it was so that the works of God might be displayed in him (John 9:1–3 New American Standard Bible 1995).

Often when the subject of God comes up, people try to change the topic because they are uncomfortable with the sin in their life. We can't have it both ways. Perhaps you are feeling uncomfortable right now as we're talking about this because you have not rightly dealt with the sin in your life through Christ's death and resurrection. Ask yourself honestly: is that working in your favor? Stand back thirty thousand feet and really examine your life. Search your heart and mind and compare it to Christ's life, which is how you will be judged. Always remember, Christians who share the Gospel and the love of Christ with you are not your enemies, Satan is!

I believe when we experience those times when everything invariably goes wrong, we struggle because we're looking at it from the wrong point of view. We begin from the premise that life is owed to us rather than the gift that it is. We tend to blame God in an attempt to bring Him down to our level—as if He messed up somehow. The truth is that mankind disobeyed God's direct command and we have been experiencing the painful results of that decision ever since.

Refuting Scripture is like denying an X-ray that is clearly pointing out a problem. This is clear denial, and I encourage you to pray and ask God to peel away the scales that have you blinded to His truth. Stop listening to all the lies and read God's Holy Word instead. Then simply apply the truth in faith to every experience you go through believing that God has your best interest at hand.

Living in a paralyzed body causes you to think outside the box. Especially the one they could have just put you in. When I imagine being dead or staring into a ceiling all these years, I am grateful that it was just a spinal cord injury that I suffered and not something far more serious. This was my wakeup call. This was my precious opportunity to reconsider all of life. It changed the path I was on before it was too late.

At some point, we all have to decide who we are living our lives for, and exactly what that means. Is your heart in the right place today, or have you sold your soul to the devil? That's not just an old cliché, it's a reality that we all must face. You see, when we wake up from the fog we've been living in, it's amazing how clear things become. When I began to read the Word of God, I discovered two truths that really resonated with me. The first was that He promises us He will never give us more than we can handle. He also promises that He will never leave us nor forsake us. This is His guarantee to us, and I for one believe Him. Through the indwelling power of the Holy Spirit, He has never given me more than I could handle. That is the key. The idea is to learn to live in the promises of God and not in man.

This story isn't about what man is able to accomplish. We are talking about the source of true hope and promise. And that is the working power of the Holy Spirit that is available to you the moment you become born again. It was through this experience that I began to see my need for God. This is where I stopped caring about what other people thought, and I began to concern myself with what God had to say about me instead.

Think of all the words that have come out of your mouth over the years. We've all said things that we later regretted. And what about the things you didn't say but felt in your heart? What about all the thoughts you've had that were never expressed openly or honestly? This is not about imparting guilt. It's about facing reality before a Holy and Just God on judgement day. It's time for us all to wake up and get super serious about all this!

Our minds are hostile toward God. The truth is, we don't want anything to do with Him because we're still trying to hide our sin from Him. This is exactly what Adam and Eve did in the Garden right before they were told to leave God's presence. So where does this leave us today? Well, thankfully, not without hope. God took the initiative while we were still yet sinners and loved us in spite of our sin. There wasn't anything good in us that attracted Him to us. It was all about God's amazing grace when He reached down to save us from our sin:

¹ Now there was a man of the Pharisees, named Nicodemus, a ruler of the Jews; ² this man came to Jesus by night and said to Him, "Rabbi, we know that You have come from God *as* a teacher; for no one can do these signs that You do unless God is with him." ³ Jesus answered and said to him, "Truly, truly, I say to you, unless one is born again he cannot see the kingdom of God."

⁴ Nicodemus said to Him, "How can a man be born when he is old? He cannot enter a second time into his mother's womb and be born, can he?" ⁵ Jesus answered, "Truly, truly, I say to you, unless one is born of water and the Spirit he cannot enter into the kingdom of God. ⁶ That which is born of the flesh is flesh, and that which is born of the Spirit is spirit. ⁷ Do not be amazed that I said to you, 'You must be born again.' ⁸ The wind blows where it wishes and you hear the sound of it, but do not know where it comes from and where it is going; so is everyone who is born of the Spirit."

⁹ Nicodemus said to Him, "How can these things be?" ¹⁰ Jesus answered and said to him, "Are you the teacher of Israel and do not understand these things? ¹¹ Truly, truly, I say to you, we speak of what we know and testify of what we have seen, and you do not accept our testimony. ¹² If I told you earthly things and you do not believe, how will you believe if I tell you heavenly things? ¹³ No one has ascended into heaven, but He who descended from heaven: the Son of Man. ¹⁴ As Moses lifted up the serpent in the wilderness, even so must the Son of Man be lifted up; ¹⁵ so that whoever believes will in Him have eternal life.

¹⁶ "For God so loved the world, that He gave His only begotten Son, that whoever believes in Him shall not perish, but have eternal life. ¹⁷ For God did not send the Son into the world to judge the world, but that the world might be saved through

Him. [18] He who believes in Him is not judged; he who does not believe has been judged already, because he has not believed in the name of the only begotten Son of God. [19] This is the judgment, that the Light has come into the world, and men loved the darkness rather than the Light, for their deeds were evil. [20] For everyone who does evil hates the Light, and does not come to the Light for fear that his deeds will be exposed. [21] But he who practices the truth comes to the Light, so that his deeds may be manifested as having been wrought in God."

[22] After these things Jesus and His disciples came into the land of Judea, and there He was spending time with them and baptizing. [23] John also was baptizing in Aenon near Salim, because there was much water there; and *people* were coming and were being baptized— [24] for John had not yet been thrown into prison.

[25] Therefore there arose a discussion on the part of John's disciples with a Jew

about purification. ²⁶ And they came to John and said to him, "Rabbi, He who was with you beyond the Jordan, to whom you have testified, behold, He is baptizing and all are coming to Him." ²⁷ John answered and said, "A man can receive nothing unless it has been given him from heaven. ²⁸ You yourselves are my witnesses that I said, 'I am not the Christ,' but, 'I have been sent ahead of Him.' ²⁹ He who has the bride is the bridegroom; but the friend of the bridegroom, who stands and hears him, rejoices greatly because of the bridegroom's voice. So this joy of mine has been made full. ³⁰ He must increase, but I must decrease.

³¹ "He who comes from above is above all, he who is of the earth is from the earth and speaks of the earth. He who comes from heaven is above all. ³² What He has seen and heard, of that He testifies; and no one receives His testimony. ³³ He who has received His testimony has set his seal to *this*, that God is true. ³⁴ For He whom God

has sent speaks the words of God; for He gives the Spirit without measure. [35] The Father loves the Son and has given all things into His hand. [36] He who believes in the Son has eternal life; but he who does not obey the Son will not see life, but the wrath of God abides on him." (John 3:1–36 New American Standard Bible 1995).

We don't need a PhD to figure this out. What we need is a dose of humility. Look around you. *We live in a sinful, fallen, cursed world.* Is it any wonder that life is full of continuous suffering and turmoil? Without God's grace working in our lives, there is no hope for any of us, no matter who you are or how much wealth or power you may have at the moment. It's not going to save you any more than the tooth fairy will. Do you still believe in Santa Clause? No, of course not. Why? Because it's all make-believe, and so are Satan's lies and schemes and it's time to be set free once and for all and live a Christlike life.

If you keep hitting the same pothole in front of your house year after year, whose fault is it? We live in Pennsylvania. When the weather changes in the fall, you can feel a distinct difference in the temperature. Once it happens, you don't have to walk outside every day for a month before you remember to grab your jacket on your way out the door. It becomes automatic. You do it without even thinking about it. We all have a free will to decide for ourselves. How intentional are you being about making changes in your life? Are you moving in the right direction, or are you still being deceived? If you only had six months to live, how long would it take you to make the needed changes you know you need to make? Would it take another month to figure it out? Or would you need the whole time before you got serious about it?

> [5] But if any of you lacks wisdom, let him ask of God, who gives to all generously and without reproach, and it will be given to him (James 1:5 New American Standard Bible 1995).

Wisdom is the ability to discern or judge what is true and right. A person can be knowledgeable without being wise. God wants us to have knowledge of Him and what He expects, but if we do not apply it correctly, it doesn't convert to wisdom—a trait needed to live a successful life.

Anybody can decide to live a defeated life and be very successful at it. It's easy to look around the world today and get discouraged about your future if that's all you're looking at. That is why you shouldn't place your hope in the things that are fleeting. Our lives don't stop after paralysis or whatever else you may be going through. There is real hope for everyone no matter what your situation may be—as long as you have placed your faith and trust in God Almighty. Simply continue to focus on Him, the person of Jesus Christ, and not on your current condition or present circumstances, even if it's life threatening. If you are a true born-again Christian, then you have nothing to be concerned about. Absent from the body, present with the Lord! Get excited! We haven't seen anything yet!

> [18] For I consider that the sufferings of this present time are not worthy to be compared with the glory that is to be revealed to us (Romans 8:18 New American Standard Bible 1995).

Without faith, we would have no hope at all, and maybe that's where you're at today. A person's hope boils down to a belief in something, whatever that may be. This is what ultimately motivates a person to do what he or she does. For some of us, it's a belief in Jesus Christ. But for others, it may be a belief in self or mankind. Some people believe they themselves are a god. And yet for others, their hope is in a new technology that will hopefully save everyone who does not believe in the One True God.

When you think about it, life here on earth is very short. Our lives are either kind of a tease and that's it, or there's life after this life. Do you really believe we are dependent on man's development of technology to save us, or is God real and therefore in charge?

As our lives begin to take shape and we become responsible for our actions, we must answer these fundamental questions. If we're dependent on man, then we're all in serious trouble. On the other hand, if God really does exist, as our own conscience bears witness, and by looking at all of creation around us, does it really make sense that God would create all of this, including you and I, only to live a short time, and then cease to exist?

When a person's understanding changes from what they thought was true, it can create an opportunity to look at life from a whole new perspective. For me, it wasn't until I came to know Christ as my Savior and Lord. That's when I started to really enjoy and appreciate life with a new understanding of who God was, and what my life meant to Him. It started when God began to open my eyes to see His Glory. Since then, I have never been alone or doubtful of God's presence at work in my life.

> [16] Therefore we do not lose heart, but though our outer man is decaying, yet

our inner man is being renewed day by day. [17] For momentary, light affliction is producing for us an eternal weight of glory far beyond all comparison, [18] while we look not at the things which are seen, but at the things which are not seen; for the things which are seen are temporal, but the things which are not seen are eternal (2 Corinthians 4:16–18 New American Standard Bible 1995).

As hard as it may be for some people to believe, I really don't see myself as being paralyzed. With God, you can know that He will use your life circumstances for His purposes and that gives us ultimate meaning in life. This is what should motivate you to press on when life seems impossible. As the often-quoted passages say:

[26] And looking at them Jesus said to them, "With people this is impossible, but with God all things are possible." (Matthew 19:26 New American Standard Bible 1995).

[13] I can do all things through Him who strengthens me (Philippians 4:13 New American Standard Bible 1995).

Have you ever met someone who truly enjoys life?

Someone who just seems to bounce out of bed in the morning, as if they knew something you didn't? Then there are those who just seem to be hanging in there, as if something was missing from their lives. In many cases, the latter group only seem to be happy when their circumstances are favorable. It's usually whether the stock market is up, or if the sun is shining. It's the ongoing debate of whether your cup is half full or half empty.

I believe because of this limited view of life, that many people miss the real reason we're here. I believe those who conform to this lifestyle of thinking are not truly happy because their happiness is solely dependent on their favorable circumstances. True joy can only come from contentment that is experienced in spite of our external circumstances. In other words, happiness can only come from within, and that can only come from being at peace with God.

True joy in life reaches down into the deepest part of our human experience. It far surpasses human thought or understanding and can only come from knowing God in the way He intended man to know Him. It will never be experienced through manmade religions and the worship of false gods. These were all designed by man to serve man within their fallen nature. Satan is having a field day, and mankind is missing the boat.

Circumstantial happiness is similar to masking pain with a pill. We know the pain is still there, but with the help of pain killers, a person doesn't notice it as much, and can continue with less discomfort. At first it seems to be a temporary fix to the problem. But unless it is addressed properly, the issue will remain just below the surface. Many people who struggle to make sense of life do so because they continue to mask their doubts and fears with countless other distractions. This is by design: rather than face reality and admit that God is real, they consciously suppress the truth.

When people are dependent on certain conditions to feel good about their lives, they are really not in control at all. They are being controlled as a result of their willingness to surrender to such a way of life. Because of this, they are missing that necessary and important part of life that gives real meaning and value to our existence. They are actually setting themselves up for a lifetime of frustration and disappointment. And when their temporary pain medicine wears off, they quickly run to get another fix, or the pain of life becomes too much to bear. I call this a lifestyle of denial. This life has a way of wearing us down, and in the process, we begin to search our hearts for meaning beyond the basic things of life. Once all the superficial things in life are stripped away, and life is understood to be much more than just material things, our lives begin to take on a whole new meaning.

It's concerning how some people will spend decades planning for their retirement and work tirelessly to save for their later years, but then fail to contemplate death. It's not that they don't think about it. It's because it's an uncomfortable subject most people don't want to talk about. Instead of raising the bar, and keep raising the bar based on God's Word, they are content with a lower standard that doesn't cost them anything—or so they think.

So, I ask you, if you find yourself trying to hang on to life, what is it that you're trying to hang on to? Is it in things that eventually fade away? Do you have a plan for your future beyond retirement, or have you placed all your assurance in wishful thinking? What are you going to do when you have to admit that yes, all good things must come to an end. Now you're staring down a six-foot hole and your faith has always been in something that you could purchase or hold on to.

This is where most people just continue to kick the can down the road. Do you realize your number could be called today? This is exactly what happened to me. Except I couldn't kick the can any longer. I was forced to sit back and rethink my life. I can't begin to tell you how grateful I am today! Praise God's Holy name!

We can all relate to the natural human drive we experience as we struggle to get established in this life. Along our journey we take on various interests that occupy us for a time, but we never seem to be fully satisfied. As our lives begin to take different turns, we start to ask ourselves the question, "What's the point of all this?" When we are going through difficult times, we have to be willing to ask the hard-hitting questions. The problem begins and continues when we try to fill our lives with things that entertain us rather than finding our fulfillment in serving a Holy God. Somehow, we think the plan we have for our lives is far better than the plan God Himself has for us. Consider what you are thinking right now as you read this. Search your heart. Be completely honest with yourself. Your eternal destiny is what is at stake! Are you telling God you are not interested in what He desires for your life? Could that be the real reason your life feels so off track?

I believe most people don't realize it's through the harder times in life that we have the potential to grow the most. That includes first and foremost where you stand with God. The key is to be willing to receive the truth when it becomes evident to you. This can only come from God Himself. We just need to do ourselves a favor and get out of the way and let God bring healing to our lives, our marriages, our families, our neighborhoods, and all the nations around the world.

Perhaps today you are realizing that you're only going to get so far by doing things in your own strength. Maybe now you're concluding that no matter how hard you've tried, things just haven't turned out the way you had hoped. Well, believe it or not, this can actually be one of the best things that has ever happened to you.

Sometimes on our journey to discover the true meaning of life, we realize we have far more questions than answers. I think everybody experiences this sooner or later. One of the signs of this is that your own thoughts and feelings will have less and less influence on your life as you continue to search for real truth.

Remember, as you start to look around for reasons to believe in something to guide your life, don't settle for a quick fix. Be willing to dig deep. Ask the hard questions that a lot of people don't like to ask. Keep in mind that just because you don't like the answers at first, it doesn't make them any less true. Like any worthwhile relationship, your belief system will be tested, and the validity of those beliefs will be verified over time, so don't be afraid of the truth—faithfully follow it wherever it takes you.

The Apostle Paul describes the natural man's dilemma:

[14] But a natural man does not accept

the things of the Spirit of God, for they are foolishness to him; and he cannot understand them, because they are spiritually appraised (1 Corinthians 2:14 New American Standard Bible 1995).

You are incapable of discerning the things of God without His help. And once God becomes involved in your life, what more do you need?

Are you starting to see that our lives have a much deeper meaning and purpose than you may have initially thought? There are many biblical reasons to believe our present lives will be reflected throughout all eternity. Therefore, we should consider every life precious and meaningful. Spiritual discernment is what is needed for a person to accurately understand the differences between truth and Satan's lies and perversion.

When you think about your life, have you ever felt like you've been duped by what the world promotes as success? Where do you personally stand with God today? This should be first and foremost on your mind. Are you heading in the right direction, or are you continuing to go down the hopeless road of denial?

Perhaps you are ready to change the way you're living and to step away from the crowd and do something extraordinary with your life.

Real change requires real sacrifice. You cannot transform your heart and renew your mind by continuing to do the same old thing. It doesn't work that way. It never has, and it never will.

There is an old saying. "If you always do what you have always done, you will always get what you have always gotten. And, if you want what you have never had, you have to do what you have never done. And the definition of insanity, is to keep doing things the same way, expecting a different result."

Life can be very difficult at times, and it can seem downright impossible at other times. If more people were honest with themselves, they would admit they fear for their future. We've all experienced things in life that have challenged our faith, and without real hope, things can get bleak fast. So where does a person find hope to keep going? It's been said, "Five years from now, you will be the same person you are today with the exception of the books you've read, and the people you've met." This has never been truer than in the case of the Holy Bible, and the One True God found in Scripture! Get excited!

When we really stop to consider the true meaning of our lives, it's far greater than what we've reduced it to. It's easy to grow up to believe true happiness is all about attaining wealth, fame, and prestige. But is that really the case? Logic tells us a certain amount of income is necessary to meet our needs in order to live a healthy, comfortable life. But the one question each of us needs to answer is this: is accumulating wealth the purpose of life?

If our lives only amounted to, "He who dies with the most toys wins," then we would have nothing to lose. For the sake of our conversation, let's imagine for a minute that that's the case. Let's imagine a world where the extent of our lives was to experience as much pleasure as possible before dying.

Let's say you just won the jackpot and you're an instant millionaire. You now live in a beautiful home on a lake, complete with a forty foot boat that's accompanied by the most beautiful person on earth that lives to meet your every need. Sounds great, right? And a mile from your luxurious beach house is your world-class business which is located right next door to the local investment banker where you have invested your fortune. The news is in, and sales have exceeded all expectations, and your company has been listed on the New York Stock Exchange at fifty dollars per share. Things couldn't be any better, right?

Besides being able to purchase many things at the drop of a hat, you now have some temporary assurances that you can live a more comfortable life for an uncertain amount of time. But this still doesn't solve your greatest problem, and that is, then what? What's going to happen after you've spent your whole life trying to control the here and now? At the end of your life, you will have to ask yourself, what was it all for? Are you still going to believe your life plan was better than the plan and purposes God had for you?

If you apply the same business practices that a successful businessman would in running his business, you would be wise to consider all the unknowns that can happen. This would include your personal life as well. The man or woman that ignores these things end up paying a big price. In the end, someone else will end up inheriting all your wealth and you won't even have the satisfaction of knowing how your fortune will be managed after you're long gone and forgotten. Many years ago, I heard a story about a very successful businessman who watched his son unscrupulously mismanage decades of hard work and sacrifice.

Remember, wealth in itself is not a bad thing. But it's how you choose to manage it. When we allow wealth to control us by believing the more we can accumulate, the more we will feel secure or satisfied in life, we are feeding the idea that the value of our lives amounts to a brief life of indulgences. This is what you would call a short-sighted investment plan. Scripture is clear on this:

¹⁰ He who loves money will not be satisfied with money, nor he who loves abundance with its income. This too is vanity (Ecclesiastes 5:10 New American Standard Bible 1995).

¹⁰ For the love of money is a root of all sorts of evil, and some by longing for it have wandered away from the faith and pierced themselves with many griefs (1 Timothy 6:10 New American Standard Bible 1995).

⁵ Make sure that your character is free from the love of money, being content with what you have; for He Himself has said, "I will never desert you, nor will I ever forsake you," (Hebrews 13:5 New American Standard Bible 1995).

To further prove my point, at the beginning of time, God never thought it necessary to provide Adam and Eve with a mansion, a Mercedes, and a million dollars in the bank. They were perfectly content with a precious intimate relationship with God Himself until they were deceived by Satan (much like many people in the world are today). Besides doing some farming every day, they didn't even know what clothing was. It wasn't until they disobeyed God and discovered they were naked after eating from the tree of the knowledge of good and evil. And when they did so, they used fig leaves to cover themselves up for the first time because they were ashamed and hid themselves from God. That's an example of how Holy and Pure things were before the fall of mankind. Then Satan perverted everything, and our sinful nature welcomed it.

> [5] Then the Lord saw that the wickedness of man was great on the earth, and that every intent of the thoughts of his heart was only evil continually (Genesis 6:5 New American Standard Bible 1995).

The point is, God provided Adam and Eve with everything they needed. He obviously knew their needs better than they did themselves. And when they did not obey His command, mankind lost its way, and this continues on to the present age. The intimacy Adam and Eve shared together with God before the fall is what brought them complete joy and fulfillment. It was all based on a Holy and Pure relationship that God designed for man in a Perfect and Holy state. It was never just based on their own relationship between themselves, or the unending acres and countless creatures God created for them to enjoy.

So, the question is, does a person's wealth

define who they are? Is that the end-all purpose of our lives here? Or are we who we are because God Himself opened our eyes to see His glory and has changed our heart toward the things of God? This comes down to a correct understanding of who we are through the eyes of God, and not man. You see, when a person grows in their understanding through a personal relationship with God, they experience spiritual intimacy that leads to the knowledge of God's plan for their life. And as they learn to trust in God's sovereignty, they will in faith believe God is orchestrating every detail of their life. This includes the difficult times, believing these difficulties to consist of a specific lesson for them to learn. It leads to even greater understanding and intimacy on a Christian's journey to holiness.

One of the beautiful things about this is we're all on a level playing field. God doesn't have favorites. We are all equal in His eyes, no matter what your past may be, or what your personal circumstances are at the moment.

In order to put our lives into proper perspective, in light of all eternity, we must be honest with ourselves and come to terms with a few things. The biggest issue is the denial of sin in our lives, and the wishful thinking that somehow we're going to live forever outside of God's design. We also must recognize the deception of chasing riches, which is another one of Satan's schemes.

So, whether you're rich or poor, or young or old, we must face these deceptive practices truthfully. The real truth is what you thought would bring you fulfillment in this life has never lasted very long. And as you continue to get older, you now must settle into the fact that life goes on and there's nothing you can do to slow it down. Eventually, like those who have gone before you, it will be your turn to say goodbye.

As you may have learned by now, no matter how hard you've tried to satisfy this lingering emptiness, it has never filled that void that you've always felt deep down inside. Herein lies the problem. If you happen to be a younger person today, and you haven't exhausted all your efforts, then you may not be ready to hear my message. The good news is, if you are ready to change the way you're living, no matter how old you may be, then get excited. I'm about to share with you an incredible true story of how God pulled my life out of the gutter and into His Kingdom. My life has never been so wonderful in spite of my crippling circumstances, all because of the amazing grace of God and His redemptive plan for our lives!

CHAPTER FOUR: WHAT IS YOUR CONCEPT OF GOD?

Remember when you graduated from high school and you either headed off to college or found a job. You couldn't wait to spread your wings and discover what life was all about. Maybe you believed, like most kids, that your parents were half the problem. That they were holding you back from all the fun in life. Maybe you were like I was, and you were all too eager to find out the truth for yourself.

This yearning to experience life for ourselves is not unnatural. In fact, it feeds right into our sinful nature that we are all born with. So, down the road we went to discover what life was all about. After a few years of freedom to do as we please, we discovered that life isn't all that it's cracked up to be. What we thought was our right to independence and freedom of expression turned out to be more of an experiment gone wrong. That supposed pot of gold at the end of the rainbow turned out to be more regret in a growing list of disappointments.

This freedom to express ourselves proved to be counterproductive. And now that we're older, we've been forced to spend a large amount of time and energy cleaning up the mess; exactly what our parents—in the best way they knew how—were trying to save us from. A person can spend decades trying to heal from poor decisions. And even longer than that if they lack the correct information to bring true healing and transformation.

When an individual finally concludes that there's got to be more to life than this, usually something has happened that has caused them to rethink everything. This is a good thing. It can be the beginning of something great if we don't continue to get deceived over and over again.

We will never know how much we need to change until we fully realize how lost we are in terms of our separation from God because of our sin. It directly affects everything and everyone in our lives. We are all completely lost and without hope when we come into this world, and that is why you have always felt a void that refuses to go away. I mentioned before that most people don't like to discuss the reality of God's existence and the fact that we are accountable to Him, but you will never properly address your circumstances until you do. By continuing to try to fill this emptiness with other things, you will only continue to live a life that will never be fulfilling to you in the truest sense of the matter.

This is the fork in the road that we all must face. The bottom line is that one road leads to Heaven, and the other road to hell. We have all sinned in our lives, and until you are ready to face this fact and the consequences thereof, then you will continue to live a life of confusion and disorder. There is absolutely no hope whatsoever apart from God's Grace being poured out into your life. *You need to wrap your mind around that today.* An opportunity to change the direction of your life is knocking at your door, and this is not a time to pretend like nobody's home. You can either continue to live in a delusion for another decade or two, or you can face the facts and begin to take steps toward a brighter future starting now.

So, if you're tired of life as you know it, and you're looking for a reason to keep going, then I would encourage you to cry out to God Himself to show you the truth. It's important to understand that your life will not change without the Spirit of God living in you to will and to do. That's because your nature is completely corrupt, and until you come to terms with this, you're just fooling yourself, but not really. The cry for help is summed up well in Psalm 86:

³ Be gracious to me, O Lord,

For to You I cry all day long.

⁴ Make glad the soul of Your servant,
For to You, O Lord, I lift up my soul.

⁵ For You, Lord, are good, and ready to forgive,
And abundant in lovingkindness to all who call upon You.

⁶ Give ear, O Lord, to my prayer;
And give heed to the voice of my supplications!

⁷ In the day of my trouble I shall call upon You,
For You will answer me (Psalm 86:3–7 New American Standard Bible 1995).

One of the reasons you may not want to believe there is a God, or you don't wish to acknowledge Him as Lord in your life, is because you're still in love with your sin. Up until now, you may have been living a lifestyle that is contrary to Scripture. The first thing you need to do is take a long in-depth look inside the Word of God and be ready to face reality. We all know what sin is, and we all know we're guilty of it in our lives. It's time to own it by sincerely asking God for His forgiveness and turn in the opposite direction!

The real question is, are you at the point where sin is no longer fun to you? Maybe your lifestyle has finally taken its toll and you have exhausted your efforts to find meaning in life without God. Maybe you've come to realize how true peace in life has escaped you over the years, whether it is in your own heart and mind, or between you and your spouse and your precious children. Maybe today is the day you're ready to get off this worldly merry-go-round. Maybe now you're ready to acknowledge that undeniable void inside of you that has existed since you were born. Think about the following verse for a minute:

> [13] No temptation has overtaken you but such as is common to man; and God is faithful, who will not allow you to be tempted beyond what you are able, but with the temptation will provide the way of escape also, so that you will be able to endure it (1 Corinthians 10:13 New American Standard Bible).

It's no secret all of mankind is struggling with the same thing. We all need to come to the only solution to the problem, and that is we need God's forgiveness of our sins, and we need His help to heal us from the inside out. In order to do that, we must place our faith in Christ's death and Resurrection and become born again.

> [24] Then Jesus said to His disciples, "If

anyone wishes to come after Me, he must deny himself, and take up his cross and follow Me. [25] For whoever wishes to save his life will lose it; but whoever loses his life for My sake will find it. [26] For what will it profit a man if he gains the whole world and forfeits his soul? Or what will a man give in exchange for his soul? [27] For the Son of Man is going to come in the glory of His Father with His angels, and will then repay every man according to his deeds (Matthew 16:24 New American Standard Bible 1995).

Ever since the fall of mankind, people have searched for the true meaning of life. Well, look no further, for Jesus says: "Whoever loses his life for My sake, will find it." Christ is the heart and center of life, and without Him, you simply would not exist. When people lose hope in life and they struggle for meaning and purpose, they often look to drugs, alcohol, or other things to numb themselves. This approach has never helped anybody. All it does is waste precious time that you can never get back. As a result, relationships with your spouse, children, family, friends, neighbors, and God Himself suffer.

I encourage you today to give life to your

soul by repenting of your sins and head in a new direction. Jesus asked the question: do you wish to save your life, and are you willing to lose your life for My sake? That is the only way you will ever find true meaning in life, and that will only happen when you place your faith in Christ alone for your Salvation. You can go on dabbling in a lot of different things as you try to find answers that will accommodate the sin in your life, or you can embrace the truth today and humble yourself before God and begin to experience real transformation. As the second book of Timothy states:

> [16] All Scripture is inspired by God and profitable for teaching, for reproof, for correction, for training in righteousness;
>
> [17] so that the man of God may be adequate, equipped for every good work (2 Timothy 3:16–17 New American Standard Bible 1995).

For the first twenty-six years of my life, I wandered from one thing to the next looking for some sense of purpose. Perhaps today you are coming to the same conclusion I did after God opened my eyes to see my need for Him. I began to realize that there is much more to life than just having a great weekend, or a perfect job with a view, or a beautiful home on a lake. These things are all nice, but they are really only meant to meet our superficial needs, and pale in comparison to a personal, Holy, Righteous, intimate relationship with God and His eternal kingdom.

When I became a quadriplegic in July of 1988, I began to get a glimpse of just how precious life really is. The Bible says we are made in the image of God. He doesn't waste anything, not even a paralyzed person confined to a wheelchair. There are important lessons for us to learn no matter what our situation may be. My life as a C5 quadriplegic does not consist of who I was, but who I have become in Christ. We were made in the image of God Himself, and not out of some blob of tissue like some would have you believe, or that your great, great, great, great grandparents came from monkeys. It is just not true.

> [26] Then God said, "Let Us make man in Our image, according to Our likeness; and let them rule over the fish of the sea and over the birds of the sky and over the cattle and over all the earth, and over every creeping thing that creeps on the earth." (Genesis 1:26 New American Standard Bible).

It's not enough to just have a concept of God if

your belief isn't derived from the Holy Scriptures of the Bible. There is but One True God. And there are also many false gods created by man to accommodate their sin. Guess what? It's not going to work. Unless your faith is in the One True God, your hope is empty and so is your faith. Ask yourself, why would God confuse everything by creating multiple ways to Salvation? No, God is not a God of confusion. He does everything in a logical and organized manner, and this is no different. The reality is that there is but one God and one path that leads to truth. The book of Isaiah says:

> [10] "You are My witnesses," declares the Lord,
> "And My servant whom I have chosen,
> So that you may know and believe Me
> And understand that I am He.
> Before Me there was no God formed,
> And there will be none after Me (Isaiah 43:10 New American Standard Bible).

God said, "Before Me, there was no God formed." This is a fundamental truth. There is only one God, and that is the Lord Jesus Christ. There were many false gods created by mankind after the fall to provide accommodation for man's sinful nature, and that's where we are still at today. Don't take my word for it: search it out.

Investigate it for yourself. You have to come to your own conclusions about what you really believe. Who you will serve and obey. So, I ask you, who are you going to place your faith in that will affect you for all eternity? I caution you. You don't want to put this off!

> [25] For they exchanged the truth of God for a lie, and worshiped and served the creature rather than the Creator, who is blessed forever. Amen (Romans 1:25 New American Standard Bible 1995).

> [28] There you will serve gods, the work of man's hands, wood and stone, which neither see nor hear nor eat nor smell (Deuteronomy 4:28).

Your life is very valuable to God, or He would never have died on the Cross for your sins. If it was just for me or just for you, Jesus would have still gone to the Cross. And if you don't believe that, then maybe you don't really believe what the Bible says. When God breathed life into you, He created you with a spirit that will live forever after this life is over. It is not only our present lives that we need to concern ourselves with, but our eternal state in which we will exist before you know it. We are reminded of this every time a loved one (or a friend, a neighbor, or stranger) passes away. It's going to happen. The only question is how soon before *your* number is called?

The only way to find true acceptance and joy in your life is to trust and believe that God's eternal kingdom is real. Only He can forgive you of your sins. All of God's children will rule and reign with Him forever. Stop living as if there was no hope, because there is, and it is available today to those who believe. The Bible warns us that Jesus Christ's return is imminent. Do not take time for granted.

When you begin to view life from a different perspective following your Salvation in Jesus Christ, you are now identified with Him, and your sin is forgiven forever. All the confusion you have been experiencing turns into understanding and an opportunity to use it for God's Glory. As you continue to turn your life around, instead of viewing things as a tragedy or a burden, it soon becomes part of your testimony as you minister to others. Examine the following verses as the Apostle Paul describes his new perspective on life through Christ.

> [7] But whatever things were gain to me, those things I have counted as loss for the sake of Christ. [8] More than that, I count all things to be loss in view of

the surpassing value of knowing Christ Jesus my Lord, for whom I have suffered the loss of all things, and count them but rubbish so that I may gain Christ, [9] and may be found in Him, not having a righteousness of my own derived from the Law, but that which is through faith in Christ, the righteousness which comes from God on the basis of faith, [10] that I may know Him and the power of His resurrection and the fellowship of His sufferings, being conformed to His death; [11] in order that I may attain to the resurrection from the dead (Philippians 3:7–11 New American Standard Bible 1995).

You see, Paul counted everything as loss for Christ's sake. He said nothing mattered in comparison to the surpassing knowledge of knowing Christ. And that his righteousness did not come from the law, but through faith in Christ. A righteousness that comes from God on the basis of faith so that he would know the power of His Resurrection and the fellowship of His sufferings. And through this, Paul attains Resurrection from his sinful nature and, ultimately, death.

Do you really want to transform your life?

Are you truly ready to change your identity and the way you are living today? That is what happens when you come to trust Jesus Christ as your Savior and Lord. Some people believe what I am describing as radical change, and indeed it is. Once you are identified with Christ, everything changes as you continue to grow in your new faith. The fear of the unknown fades and not even death itself will concern you any longer.

The person you are today is a result of the choices you have made, which you alone determined. It is a person's heart that leads to a decision and the consequences of life follow. Positive change only happens when you start making right decisions based on God's Word. This will guide you down a straight and narrow path to truth, which will set you free. Many people today have become complacent and accept the ordinary instead of the extraordinary. People are losing hope because they have looked for meaning and purpose in all the wrong places and in all the wrong things.

We all experience various difficulties in this life. And we would all agree that we naturally see trials as disappointments or setbacks rather than opportunities for personal growth. If you had asked me before my injury to volunteer to become a quadriplegic, I would have run in the opposite direction. I am not suggesting paralysis or anything like it is necessary or a desired lifestyle, of course. But what I am saying is that difficult circumstances, whatever they may be, have the potential benefit of pointing us to our Creator. God has a plan for each of our lives, and when that time is up, He will pull the plug—but not a moment sooner.

Instead of responding in the same old way, why not take a different path. To begin with, don't view your current situation as permanent. It's not. Things change based on your view of life. If you are a true born-again Christian, the Bible says, "I can do all things through Him who strengthens me," (Philippians 4:13 New American Standard Bible 1995). Secondly, the Bible says, "... absent from the body and to be home with the Lord," (2 Corinthians 5:8). So, ask yourself, is your cup half full, or half empty? When you learn to trust in the Holy Spirit, your cup overflows. You see, life isn't over. Not at all. It is just the beginning. Remember the Apostle Paul—he walked away every single time until it was time for him to go home.

So, the one percent chance that doctors gave me to live implies that ninety-nine percent of me was ready to pass into eternity and I was completely powerless to stop it. I used to wonder why I survived my accident and others were not as fortunate. It used to be a mystery to me, but that has all changed along with many other misconceptions I had about life. It certainly was not that I deserved to live more than someone else, or that I was a better person than they were.

When it comes to pain and suffering, yes there is the physical side to it, but there is a spiritual side as well. If you are a Christian seeking to grow in your faith, it's the side effects of trials that can really bless your life. When we go through difficulties, it disrupts our lives and often causes strife between family members. This is when we can apply Scripture immediately to our situation, and trust God to cause everything to work together for good! Therefore, trials become steppingstones to great understanding and sanctification to the person who views and responds to the opportunity by faith. This is exactly why the trials that we go through are such a wonderful blessing. It is an endless opportunity throughout our lives to reverse the effects of our sinful nature and be transformed back into Christlikeness. As a Christian, this is priceless!

One of the greatest mistakes we can make is to think we're in charge, and that it's really human beings who are sovereign and not God. The truth is nobody really believes that, but for some, they try to convince themselves and others so they can play god. This is very foolish and, frankly, a silly notion. To prove my point, let's do a short experiment. Hold your breath for ten minutes. You see? That didn't even take five minutes. The point is you do not control your breathing any more than you can control when you come into this world, or when you exit this world. The truth is God created you and you simply would not exist unless He chose to give you life, and everything else is nonsense.

One of the biggest problems with trying to create meaning and purpose in life apart from God is that there is no life without God. Do not be deceived here. This is a failed approach and will frankly end in your destruction and eternal separation from God forever.

Once again, the Bible tells us that the reason people try to deny God's existence is because they choose sin over God. And because they love their sin more than God, they rationalize about His existence and attempt to block their conscience that God graciously wired us with. Then they pretend to live in their fallen state of depravity without the constant guilt and shame accompanying their lawless lifestyle. This approach to life has a one hundred percent failure rate.

> [19] This is the judgment, that the Light has come into the world, and men loved the darkness rather than the Light, for
>
> their deeds were evil. [20] For everyone who does evil hates the Light, and does not come to the Light for fear that his deeds will be exposed (John 3:19–20

New American Standard Bible 1995).

As you can clearly see below, all of our deeds are going to come to light.

> [17] For nothing is hidden that will not become evident, nor anything secret that will not be known and come to light (Luke 8:17 New American Standard Bible 1995).

If you don't think sin is serious, you need to think again. Sin is the very reason Christ died. Take a minute and think about that statement. God died. That is amazing to contemplate. And He did it for your sin and mine. And to rationalize this fact for a few decades of so-called fun compared to all eternity is very foolish. There is no misunderstanding about this. If you're living in sin, your life needs to be exposed for what it really is so you can deal with it at the Cross:

> [23] for all have sinned and fall short of the glory of God (Romans 3:23 New American Standard Bible 1995).

The definition of self-righteousness is confidence in one's own righteousness. If we could produce righteousness by ourself, Christ could have bypassed the Cross. Because of our sinful nature, we believe we are or can be righteous in ourselves, which is completely unbiblical, and we all know it! It's time to admit it and acknowledge our sin before God. Humble yourself. Tomorrow could be too late.

Before my injury, my whole approach to life was very shortsighted. Frankly, I was completely ignorant of the truth. I had no consideration of the more important questions about life such as, "Where did I come from? What is my purpose here? Where do I go when I die?" This really gets at the heart of the issue. And that is that I need to learn a lot more about these things so I can make wiser decisions moving forward. One of the reasons some people don't take this serious enough is because they are not truly interested in what God wants for their lives, which is to be Holy and Righteous. They have become content with sin. Is that where you are today? Or are you ready to live the rest of your life serving Christ, and fulfilling your ministry as you model and share His love with everyone you have opportunity with? God is not going to force you or anyone else to love Him! Our free will, by design, exposes where we really stand.

When we're young, we tend to believe that we don't have to concern ourselves with death. And when we see others die or are killed, we rationalize and say that it's not going to happen to us, so we put off these conversations until another time. But is that a wise thing to do?

Common sense says no! When you were born, neither the doctor nor the hospital handed your parents a warranty promising a long and painless life.

We all need to come to realize how ridiculous Satan's lies are, and how he tries to twist everything. He is trying to undermine our hope and faith in God, and therefore our relationship with Him, and all the love and blessings that He has prepared for those who love Him! Satan doesn't want us to discover how truly wonderful God is, and how He loves and cares for us perfectly!

The truth is, we have all taken the bait, and it has greatly affected our lives, including all our loved ones! Don't be fooled any longer. God defeated Satan on the Cross. Jesus said, "It is finished!" We all need to stop listening to Satan's lies and learn to trust and obey our Lord as we take every thought captive to the obedience of Christ.

> [30] Therefore when Jesus had received the sour wine, He said, "It is finished!" And He bowed His head and gave up His spirit (John 19:30 New American Standard Bible 1995).

The deception of riches gives us a convoluted picture of what really brings true joy and contentment to a person's life. We can all spend an immense amount of time and energy chasing temporary indulgencies in this world, or we can submit to God and follow Him according to His perfect will and purpose wherever that road may lead. He will then provide all our needs and much more!

> [7] "Ask, and it will be given to you; seek, and you will find; knock, and it will be opened to you. [8] For everyone who asks receives, and he who seeks finds, and to him who knocks it will be opened. [9] Or what man is there among you who, when his son asks for a loaf, will give him a stone? [10] Or if he asks for a fish, he will not give him a snake, will he? [11] If you then, being evil, know how to give good gifts to your children, how much more will your Father who is in heaven give what is good to those who ask Him! (Matthew 7:7–11 New American Standard Bible 1995).

The larger question here will always remain: what will happen to your spirit after you leave this world? This isn't based on a person's feelings. This is about our sin and where we stand with God in terms of His forgiveness. If you don't have peace in your heart that heaven is in your future based on Christ's death and Resurrection for your sin, then you need to ask God for mercy and forgiveness and repent. Stop sinning and live a Christlike life. Pray for wisdom. Follow the Holy Spirit's lead throughout your day. Trust God's Word. Praise Him and thank Him! Get excited about the rest of your life! Press on.

When we fail to apply God's truth that is specifically designed to set us free, what do we expect? That's where I was before my injury. But by the grace of God, I not only survived to live another day, but I also learned the key to life and have discovered true purpose and meaning for our existence here and throughout all eternity. God's amazing grace is absolutely incredible! Embrace it today. Tomorrow could be too late.

This life is half over before you know it, and the second half seems to go faster than the first. Jesus Christ (through the power of the Holy Spirit) has given me the ability and desire to live beyond my circumstances with supernatural love, joy, and peace that is not based on what I am going through, or how I may be feeling at the moment—but rather in God's Holiness which is demonstrated to us through His faithfulness to His Word. Does that mean that I am perfect every day? No, but I am fully committed to keep growing in Christlikeness every single day that God grants me to live. We don't have a day to waste! Search your heart. Look at your schedule. How are you spending your time? Is God's Glory at the heart and center of everything you do?

If you are a Christian, do you honor the Lord's Day each week? I remember Michelle and I's first year of marriage. We were clueless and totally unprepared. We ended up separating for a couple of months. When we got back together, we renewed our vows in our living room. On Sundays I would spend some time watching games during football and basketball season. The problem is that there is not enough time in the day for everything, so I had to decide what was most important. It was God and our marriage, of course.

> [24] "Therefore everyone who hears these words of Mine and acts on them, may be compared to a wise man who built his house on the rock. [25] And the rain fell, and the floods came, and the winds blew and slammed against that house; and yet it did not fall, for it had been founded on the rock. [26] Everyone who hears these words of Mine and does not act on them, will be like a foolish man who built his house on the sand. [27] The rain fell, and the floods came, and the winds blew and slammed against that

house; and it fell—and great was its fall." (Matthew 7:24–27 New American Standard Bible 1995).

Well, I did the unthinkable at the time, and quit watching nearly all sports games for five years. Guess what, it didn't kill me. When the five years had come to an end, I watched a few games here and there, and decided I would just track the score on my laptop to see who won. I also occasionally watched a few highlights of my favorite team on Monday; a difference between fifteen minutes and three hours. That adds up to a serious amount of time over the course of a decade, let alone our lifetime.

Now I don't even bother to track the score anymore. It is not important compared to fulfilling your ministry while we only have a limited opportunity to do so! Remember, you can never ever get this time back! I'm not saying some recreation isn't helpful and refreshing. It is. But we need to weigh each day and prayerfully decide what's most important, so we don't live to regret it later.

As born-again Christians, our will should be God's will. This is all about making wise decisions based on Scripture, which is the final authority on all matters of faith and practice. Honoring God and His Word must be our daily passion! We should submit and obey Him simply because that is what He commands. When we listen and do what He says, our lives are blessed continually. When we rebel against Him and His Word, we stay stuck in our sin and the results of those decisions. This is yet another scheme from the devil, and we the Church are buying into it. It's time we all earnestly repent and turn back to God!

> [42] saying, "Father, if You are willing, remove this cup from Me; yet not My will, but Yours be done." (Luke 22:42 New American Standard Bible).

Following Christ's example above, are you willing to do God's will in place of your own desires? Have you personally come to a place in your walk with God that you are willing to completely die to self? When we as Christians get to Heaven, will not every day be the Lord's Day? Then why not commit to do so beginning this week? As Hebrews says:

> [24] and let us consider how to stimulate one another to love and good deeds, [25] not forsaking our own assembling together, as is the habit of some, but encouraging one another; and all the more as you see the day drawing near (Hebrew 10:24–25 New American Standard Bible).

God intended the Lord's Day to be a time of refreshing! To celebrate Christ's life and all that He has done for us. Thank Him over and over for your Salvation. Break bread and enjoy precious fellowship together. We should come together to pray. To read God's Word. Then share with others all that God has so graciously taught us. Let's not rob ourselves of that, which is exactly what Satan encourages us to do. Instead, let's inspire one another, and praise God for all that He is doing in our lives! Give Him all your love and appreciation. After all, He did die to pay the penalty for our sins. All eternity will not be enough time to show our full appreciation. Men, it's time to honor the Lord's Day and train it into others, which includes the next generation. Children everywhere today desperately need our leadership and are crying out for help. Compare them to time spent watching a ballgame. Are you even going to care who won or lost a day or two later?

If you're not already, it's time to honor God by honoring the Lord's Day. It's time to get serious about every single day God gives us!

God designed the Lord's Day to be a special day for families, friends, and neighbors to enjoy His presence. To support and encourage each other. We should be spending the day persuading others of their need for Christ, or their need to keep growing in His likeness. Look around the world. People are hurting. Everyone needs the hope of the Gospel! Christ is our only hope! Share the good news with others. Plant a seed and keep watering it. It's also very important to share communion each month. It reminds us of the tremendous price Christ paid for each of us when He willingly died on the Cross for our sins. It causes us to remember our Lord's Death and Resurrection, and to watch for His glorious return. Search your heart. Examine what kind of life you've been living before eating the bread which represents His broken body that was so badly tortured that it was hardly recognizable. Understand how the wine speaks of His blood and the horrific death He experienced all for you and me.

[26] For as often as you eat this bread and drink the cup, you proclaim the Lord's death until He comes (1 Corinthians 11:26 New American Standard Bible 1995).

When I think of my life, I am completely free to enjoy God personally and intimately wherever I am through a growing relationship that consumes me, and I wouldn't want it any other way! I'm free from the bondage of sin that once had me enslaved to my old nature. I'm now free from being controlled by my circumstances, and whether everything is going well on a given day.

We can change anything and everything if we are willing to work together with God. I am no longer dependent on alcohol or drugs to help me cope with a broken life like I once was. God took all that away, and that life is behind me now, and it can be for you too. Take a look at the following verses:

> [1] Peter, an apostle of Jesus Christ, To those who reside as aliens, scattered throughout Pontus, Galatia, Cappadocia, Asia, and Bithynia, who are chosen [2] according to the foreknowledge of God the Father, by the sanctifying work of the Spirit, to obey Jesus Christ and be sprinkled with His blood: May grace and peace be yours in the fullest measure.
>
> [3] Blessed be the God and Father of our Lord Jesus Christ, who according to His great mercy has caused us to be born again to a living hope through the resurrection of Jesus Christ from the dead, [4] to obtain an inheritance which is imperishable and undefiled and will not fade away, reserved in heaven for you, [5] who are protected by the power of God through faith for a salvation ready to be revealed in the last time. [6] In this you

greatly rejoice, even though now for a little while, if necessary, you have been distressed by various trials, [7] so that the proof of your faith, being more precious than gold which is perishable, even though tested by fire, may be found to result in praise and glory and honor at the revelation of Jesus Christ; [8] and though you have not seen Him, you love Him, and though you do not see Him now, but believe in Him, you greatly rejoice with joy inexpressible and full of glory, [9] obtaining as the outcome of your faith the salvation of your souls (1 Peter 1:1–9 New American Standard Bible).

If that doesn't refresh your Spirit, you're a dead man walking. Do you realize that a lot of the time we do things just because we're feeling out of sorts? What use to be an excuse to grab a beer and spend the rest of the day trying to forget about life for a while, is now replaced with God's Love, Grace, Wisdom, and blessings. He promises to give His children the power to overcome any situation by faith in Him. With God's help every day, I have learned to thrive beyond the various difficulties that often interrupt our lives. I don't even see myself as disabled and haven't for many years because of the indwelling power of the Holy Spirit.

It was through these experiences that I discovered the greatest revelation ever known to man. I hope you will join me to discover the key to your purpose and joy that no circumstance or person will ever be able to take from you.

CHAPTER FIVE: THE DAY THINGS BEGAN TO CHANGE

It was a sunny Saturday afternoon. As I approached the curve in front of the small church I had attended Sunday school at a few times as a child, I lost control of my motorcycle. When I came to a rest, my head was wedged between the rear axle of a parked car and the pavement. To make matters even worse, I had just gotten married three weeks prior.

What must have taken about seven seconds, resulted in my whole life being completely turned upside down. This is not what we were anticipating at all. We had the idea that life was just beginning. Nobody expects tragedy, after all —but it can happen to anyone at any moment. That's how precious life is. My accident is similar to a story I heard of about a couple on their honeymoon—when the husband dove into a pool and broke his neck. His wife must have watched in horror. When you think of how precious our lives are, our approach to life should be full of grace and mercy toward one another. To love, help, support, and encourage others. To forgive as needed. Can you imagine such a world?

Have you ever thought about all the things we complain about in life? What if something like this was to happen to you? How would you begin to put your life back together? Your answers to these questions form the reasoning behind your reactions to challenges you face every day. So, where does a person discover a healthy, positive outlook when we're used to associating our happiness with our circumstances? In three words: God's Holy Bible.

> [2] You shall remember all the way which the Lord your God has led you in the wilderness these forty years, that He might humble you, testing you, to know what was in your heart, whether you would keep His commandments or not (Deuteronomy 8:2 New American Standard Bible 1995).

To have a correct perspective on life, you have to see things through God's Sovereignty and Grace. Don't skip over this too quickly or you will have missed the uniqueness of Bible-based Christianity. It's applying grace to every situation that comes up in your life, knowing God alone has the sovereign power to make it happen.

That means your circumstances plus God's unmerited favor and unlimited power changes your situation dramatically. It's the ability to persevere through difficult times with hope based on Christ's promises rather than in man.

God provides strength and comfort to every born-again believer through the indwelling power of the Holy Spirit. This enables a Christian to persevere when everything seems impossible. It is learning to rest completely in Christ regardless of how things may appear. We live by faith, not by sight. We can all simplify our lives by applying God's Word to whatever we may be going through. The key to this is to stop trying to do it yourself, and let Jesus live through you. You do this by submitting to His Word, His will, and His purpose for your life. Cry out to Him as you read the following passage:

> [28] "Come to Me, all who are weary and heavy-laden, and I will give you rest. [29] Take My yoke upon you and learn from Me, for I am gentle and humble in heart, and you will find rest for your souls. [30] For My yoke is easy and My burden is light." (Matthew 11:28–30 New American Standard Bible 1995).

Once the paramedics freed me from underneath

the car, I tried to sit up and assess the situation. When I wasn't able to, fear raced through my mind, and I realized I was in serious trouble. As you can imagine, it was terrifying. Turns out, I was not as indestructible as I thought, and neither are you if you still happen to believe that. Most people take life for granted. Fortunately for all of us, it's never too late to change our perspective on life.

As I lay there frightened for my life, a friend said the first words out of my mouth were, "Oh my God." You know, we don't usually cry out to God until we come to the end of our tether, and that's where I found myself. The length of this rope varies for all of us. For some, it can be something small that will get your attention. But for others, it takes something far greater before we humble ourselves before a Great and Mighty God.

Most of us have experienced a wake-up call at one time or another. The question is, did you respond to the alarm, or are you continuing to hit the snooze button? When a person goes through life and continues to push God to the backburner, they are putting off the central most significant and urgent issue in all of life.

As Christians, we need to be intentional to share the Gospel with those around us. We are talking about spending all eternity either in Heaven or hell. How can a person be troubled about a disease that could take their life, but not be worried about where they will spend eternity after they pass from this life? People will go immediately to their doctor's office, but they won't go to a Bible-based church and get their lives right with the Lord.

Up until my accident, I chose to push the envelope—as if I was somehow exempt from the spiritual and natural laws that govern our universe. Like many, I was out of touch with reality. In fact, reality today is not considered by many to be what is true, but often what people want to believe is true in order to accommodate the sin in their life.

Real change doesn't happen until we get serious about God. He is a reality and unavoidable to us all, and sooner or later, each one of us will have to face the fact that He is our Creator, and we are subject to Him, and not the other way around.

When I arrived at the local hospital after my crash, my X-rays confirmed what many had believed. My neck was broken, and I was paralyzed from the nipple line down. As my wife was leaving the hospital that evening, my mother-in-law said to her, "Do you realize he will never walk again?" The magnitude of such an event is incredible. It was later described as a C5 burst, C6–C7 fracture. That evening, I was airlifted to Saint Vincent's Hospital in Erie, Pennsylvania. I spent the next ten and a half months in and out of ICU four different times, and eventually I made it to rehab where I would begin the long process of learning to live life from a wheelchair.

As a young man growing up, I preferred to be on the go all the time. The problem was half the time I was busy doing all the wrong things. This often included having fun at other people's expense. You see, as someone born with a sinful nature, I loved my sin and enjoyed it half of the time. That is until it caught up with me. We have all attempted to avoid God. In fact, trying to get around God has become an American pastime that has caught up with us as a nation. This comes very natural to us from the time we were born. Even the best-intended Christians fall short of God's Glory every day. That doesn't mean we lower the bar. It means we need to ask for God's forgiveness and be disciplined enough to keep growing in our faith every moment of every day.

There are many things in life that humble us. Perhaps you are experiencing something right now that has forced you to slow down and reconsider where you stand with God. Maybe you're a Christian today and your walk with our Lord is not what it should be. Or maybe you don't know Christ as your Lord and Savior, but something has happened in your life that has caused you to see your need for Him. This is a good thing. Don't be tempted to see your circumstances or trials as just a setback to your plans. And be careful not to think that all you have to do is simply repair your state of affairs. This may be the exact conditions God is using that can lead to great understanding if your heart is ready to receive it. Is that the case? For your sake, I certainly hope so!

One of the first things I learned was when your own ability to experience life is stripped away long enough for God to get your undivided attention, great things can happen. This stripping away of our focus on self and worldly preoccupations is necessary in order to transform our lives into the person God wants us to be. Paul reminds us of this in the following verse:

> ² And do not be conformed to this world, but be transformed by the renewing of your mind, so that you may prove what the will of God is, that which is good and acceptable and perfect (Romans 12:2 New American Standard Bible 1995).

We need the mind of God guiding us through His Spirit. At that point, you are ready to grow in grace and in truth. You have to completely surrender your entire life over to God and allow His Word to dominate your life. This is not something we do naturally. That's why God often uses trials not only to get our attention, but to keep us focused on what is most important. Again, the Apostle Paul reminds Christians of who we are in Christ, and the incredible benefits and responsibilities of that calling:

> [19] Or do you not know that your body is a temple of the Holy Spirit who is in you, whom you have from God, and that you are not your own? [20] For you have been bought with a price: therefore glorify God in your body (1 Corinthians 6:19–20 New American Standard Bible 1995).

Trials come in different magnitudes of severity. Maybe you are at that point where you have exhausted all your options and you're tired of trying. This is known as coming to the end of self. This is when God is starting to soften your heart and you are beginning to listen in order to hear and obey rather than continue in your sinful rebellion.

Life has a way of catching up with us all. One way this happens is when our bodies begin to age. At this point you begin to look back over your shoulder to examine your decision-making over the years. Do you know what a midlife crisis really is? It's when you have missed God's purpose and plan for your life and time is no longer on your side. It's when reality starts to sink in, and you are forced to come to terms with the truth. This is when all the things that you perceive to be important are stripped away. Then you must decide whether you want to continue to foolishly attempt to build your own kingdom, or if you want to exchange it all for God's Kingdom and His Glory.

When this realization settles in, you start to understand that the longing you have had for meaning and purpose in life is a God-size vacuum that only He can fill. This is a huge step toward the greatest revelation in all of life. The truth is, until you experience a new birth in Christ, you will continue to struggle and will remain in your sin and be powerless to do anything about your circumstances.

So, are you listening to the alarms going off in your life that are trying to tell you that you're not right with God? With a simple prayer of faith, Paul describes the path to Salvation. The Bible says:

> [9] that if you confess with your mouth Jesus *as* Lord, and believe in your heart that God raised Him from the dead, you will be saved;
>
> [10] for with the heart a person believes, resulting in righteousness, and with the mouth he confesses, resulting in salvation (Romans 10:9–10 New

American Standard Bible 1995).

Following an earnest prayer of repentance, Christ's Spirit comes to live inside of you, filling that void for meaning in life. God tells us to search our hearts, to examine ourselves. Have you ever thought about what it is that drives you to do what you do? Have you ever asked yourself, "Is this pleasing to God?" When you look back, have all your efforts been in vain? Was it done for God's Glory or yours? When we begin to realize life is much more than what we have reduced it to, opportunity for real change is possible and that is the best thing that could ever happen to you!

I remember having all my personal privacy and dignity stripped away as a young man following my injury. As I lay there, completely naked, and dependent on others, it left me with a sense of humility I hadn't ever known before. It eventually helped me to see my need and utter dependence on God. This revelation is worth anything we go through to get it, including a serious injury.

We tend to be prideful when we're young and healthy. But when something happens that causes us to see our humanity and we're brought to our knees, we occasionally change our tune. Experiences like this begin to teach us the real meaning of life—and guess what, it's not all about you and me. This is a hard pill to swallow because we often think better of ourselves than we should, but the truth of the Cross is before all to see.

Every single day we're alive and have opportunity, we need to take account of our actions. Our lives are just a vapor, after all:

> [14] Yet you do not know what your life will be like tomorrow. You are just a vapor that appears for a little while and then vanishes away (James 4:14 New American Standard Bible 1995).

I encourage you to meditate on that verse until it sinks deep down into your soul like never before. In all reality, any number of things could happen. The world around us is changing dramatically, right before our eyes. It's time to stop putting things off as if we had all the time in the world. We don't!

Change isn't always easy. Sometimes it can be a long and painful process, such as giving up old habits. Changing your lifestyle. Healing your heart so you can improve various relationships. Discipling yourself on a daily basis. That's why most people avoid it. Some things can be changed overnight, but other changes can seem like pulling teeth. Depending on how deep a hole you have dug for yourself, you may need to work two or three times as hard to get unstuck.

So, what are some of the benefits of change? The right kind of changes will bring meaning, purpose, and value to your life. God cares and loves you more than you could ever imagine! And He wants you to know Him personally and intimately every day of your life. He loves us in a Holy and Pure way that never changes. It's exactly what we are all longing to experience.

The most important issue is to keep your eye on the prize, and never lose a biblical perspective on life. When you really start growing in your faith as a Christian, you will not want to lose that sense of peace and closeness with the Lord. It gives you a sense of identity that you may never have had with God before. This is what gives you the greatest sense of confidence in all of life because you are now identified with Jesus Christ and His Eternal Kingdom.

As I read the Bible, I've discovered that there are basically two kinds of people in the world. One is driven by his or her sinful nature and wants nothing to do with God. The other acknowledges his or her sin and seeks forgiveness from God. The unforgiven sinner is simply lost and without any real hope. The forgiven person is justified by faith in Christ and is freed from their sinful past. I remember the sense I had when I earnestly prayed for forgiveness for the first time. It was like the weight of the world was lifted and I felt clean for the first time in my life. In the following verse we're reminded of the cost of sin:

> [23] For the wages of sin is death, but the free gift of God is eternal life in Christ Jesus our Lord (Romans 6:23 New American Standard Bible 1995).

We can all remember the games we played as kids when we imagined being someone else for a minute. As we got older, we became more critical of ourselves because we felt like we didn't measure up to our own expectations, let alone the expectations of others. As a way to escape this sinking feeling, we continue to pretend in order to avoid the difficult changes that are required. If you're going to break free from unhealthy relationships and poor habits, then you're going to need some help. Someone who can support you as you work your way through it. There's nothing like a great friend and mentor. Praise God for the true Body of Christ!

Men, pretending to be John Wayne isn't going to get the job done. I dare say, old John himself didn't even believe his own press clippings. Compare him or Rambo or anyone else you would like to Jesus Christ, and you will find that we have all failed miserably. Everyone who has ever walked this earth, with the exception of Jesus Christ, has every reason to acknowledge that they are a sinner in need of God's forgiveness.

This alone will lead us to true healing. Not another drink or drug to help you zone out. And if you are still convinced that attaining riches is all you're missing, you are badly mistaken. It's all been tried, and it has failed from one century to the next.

> [9] That which has been is that which will be,
> And that which has been done is that which will be done.
> So there is nothing new under the sun (Ecclesiastes 1:9 New American Standard Bible).

Jesus Christ is who we really want to become like, and not the puffed-up, so-called role models of the world. A real man of God will lead his family with the same wisdom and graces afforded to him through Christ and not by the standards of this world. As a young man, I was beginning to follow in my dad's footsteps because that's what was modeled to me as a kid. I became an alcoholic at a young age, and it nearly ruined my life. I was more concerned with becoming what I thought other people would accept me as. All in order to belong rather than be myself because I had never seen my life as very meaningful. That continued until I became a child of God!

All the drinking was simply a way of escape,

and to numb the hurt and pain in life. It's the adult version of nursing ourselves. Is this where you are today? Are you still stuck between all the unhealed hurt and pain you've experienced? To make matters worse, I was a terrible example to my three younger brothers who eventually did much of the same. Growing up, my parents never talked about God. It wasn't that they didn't believe God was real, they just never made time for Him in their lives. They never sought Him out. It breaks my heart.

I will say one thing. At least my mom had the sense to send us to Sunday school with our babysitter. I'm sure she felt overwhelmed and hoped it would be something that could help. Following my injury, she furnished my apartment for me. She really seemed to enjoy it, and I was very grateful for her precious help.

I remember one afternoon while my mom was visiting, I opened my Bible and began to read out of the book of Matthew. Over the years, I have never forgotten the words that came out of her mouth when she said, "I never knew this stuff was in here." Sadly, she was not alone. Knowing some of the things she went through as a child and as an adult saddens me when I think of how a close relationship with God would have changed her life greatly. The comfort, strength, wisdom, and peace she could have had during those very difficult times would have made all the difference!

[15] No longer do I call you slaves, for the slave does not know what his master is doing; but I have called you friends, for all things that I have heard from My Father I have made known to you (John 15:15 New American Standard Bible 1995).

[24] A man of too many friends comes to ruin,
But there is a friend who sticks closer than a brother (Proverbs 18:24 New American Standard Bible 1995).

Life was hard growing up as a kid. I tried to escape reality by remaining in an intoxicated state half the time, not realizing what was actually going on inside of me. It seemed to work at first. When you're young, it even seems fun half the time. But what started out as social drinking with some friends as a little kid turned into a very serious matter.

If you are a Christian teenager today, pray for wisdom, which God promises to give to you abundantly. And if you are not a Christian, pray for the forgiveness of your sins, and get right with the Lord. Why make all the same old mistakes? If you could interview residents in nursing homes around the world, they too would tell you that it wasn't worth it. God has an amazing purpose and plan for your precious life. Seek Him out. You will be forever grateful!

I thank God that this has all changed today. I can honestly say that He did me a huge favor when He caused or allowed my accident to happen. It changed the path I was on, and in time, transformed my entire life—which now includes all eternity. Praise His name!

After all these years of living with a severe disability—the limitations, the pain, the suffering you go through—the various trials you experience. In spite of it all, I'm still extremely grateful. It created the conditions that helped me grow in my faith as a Christian.

After doing personal care for many years, I have come to numerous conclusions about life. One of them is that, when God created woman, He sure did us all a huge favor. I have the upmost respect for women and the way God has uniquely designed them. Life simply would not be the same if they weren't around. Unfortunately, both men and woman alike have abandoned God's perfect plan and have therefore paid a heavy price. We will continue to struggle through life until we repent of our sins and turn back to God.

> [18] Then the Lord God said, "It is not good for the man to be alone; I will make him a helper suitable for him." (Genesis 2:18

New American Standard Bible 1995).

^{22} He who finds a wife finds a good thing
And obtains favor from the Lord
(Proverbs 18:22 New American
Standard Bible).

The problems we suffer from today are in the area of true leadership. The roles designed for men too often have been relinquished to the woman in the home and this has destabilized our families. Our society is paying a huge price because it's simply against God's design. The people who are caught in the middle are suffering greatly. Women could do a much better job being a wife and a mother if they weren't forced into the sole leadership position half the time. There are also some women who have opted to forgo their original role as their husband's wife and helpmate and have created an alternative lifestyle that rejects God's will. This is also a recipe for disaster.

We as men need to step up and be accountable. *Accountability* is not a popular word today, I admit. But the sooner we all do this, the better off we will be. Men, we need to learn to become real leaders in our homes and set an example for our wives and children. Learn to love your wife as described in the Bible. Take a greater interest in your wife and children while you're alive and able to do so. If your parents failed to be a good example to you in this way, then you need to learn this from someone else. No, it's not going to be easy, but that's exactly why we all desperately need God's help. Exercise your faith and believe.

> [6] And without faith it is impossible to please Him, for he who comes to God must believe that He is and that He is a rewarder of those who seek Him (Hebrews 11:6 New American Standard Bible 1995).

The Bible addresses every issue in life, and it will give you specific answers for everything you'll ever go through. Pray and say to God, "May Your Presence be found in this place for Your Glory and Honor, dear Lord!"

The problem we are having is that people have forgotten how to pick up their Bibles and actually read *and apply the Word to their daily lives.* We have all done this and are guilty. If you are experiencing a trial that has tested you, see it as an opportunity to seriously change the direction of your life. Pick up a Bible and develop a personal relationship with God Almighty. Put your trust in Jesus Christ alone and be set free once and for all.

If you are stuck in a rut, then I challenge you to slow down and get off the rat wheel. Stop trying to keep up with the Joneses. Dare to rethink your life and where you're headed. Be uncommonly honest with yourself and others. Have the courage to step out of your comfort zone. Confess the things that have needed to be confessed and confront them at the Cross. If you have been in denial, snap out of it because tomorrow could be too late. Dare to be different from others. Where has it ever gotten you when you decided to give in to pressure and you went-along to get-along? It's all a lie from the devil himself.

You should be far more concerned with what God thinks than what people think. Image versus reality is what it amounts to. Be a man or a woman of God. If you really want to change your life, ask for some help from a good Bible-based church who would be happy to guide you to truly turn your life around. But be certain your local church is solidly Bible based! Satan has deceived many people in the Church as well. He has gone as far as to plant willing accomplices in an effort to diminish the Church and give God a black eye at the same time. The same goes with different ministries on the internet. It makes sense that the devil would do everything he can to destroy the true Church and the nuclear family.

It's a huge step in the right direction when a man admits he has made an error in his judgment. This takes faith to step up and acknowledge where we've gone wrong. This is a characteristic of true leadership.

The truth is we have all failed at life in various ways. Stop trying to pretend you're someone else, and just be yourself in Christ. If you're a husband, be a great husband. If you're a dad, be a great dad. If you're a wife, be a great wife. If you're a mom, be a great mom. If you're a pastor, a counselor, a schoolteacher, a coach, a police officer, a fireman, a paramedic, a neighbor, you name it, be all you can be. We only get one opportunity at this, and time goes by very fast!

What we need to do is begin to work through the often-painful experience of self-exploration. We all need to face the reality of our past and have the courage to confront the present as well as our future.

When a person arranges to see a doctor for something that could be life threatening, we naturally seek out someone who is very knowledgeable and experienced, right? We would also want him or her to speak the truth to us so we can make a wise decision concerning our future. That's because it can mean life or death. Well, this is also true when you consider where you stand with God, is it not?

If you are off track, the truth is the only thing that can set you free from the predicament you're in. Sin will destroy your life if you don't address it properly. Talk to others who have gone through it themselves. Once you commit to do this, you'll never look back. In fact, you will wish you had taken the opportunity long ago. Men, to put this into perspective, this is much bigger than taking a mountain, winning a battle, scoring the winning touchdown, getting a promotion, or winning the next contract. This is the first step in getting your life right with God. You're fighting the most important battle of your life, and that's for your heart and soul, and that of your precious family. Before you look anywhere else, or to anyone else, call on the name of the Lord Jesus Christ. Focus on the Resurrection Power of our Savior. It's time to get off the bench and get into the game. Leave it all on the field for God's Glory! Let's go, Church!

> [31] Yet those who wait for the Lord
> Will gain new strength;
> They will mount up with wings like eagles,
> They will run and not get tired,
> They will walk and not become weary
> (Isaiah 40:31 New American Standard Bible 1995).

CHAPTER SIX: THE GOOD NEWS

When my time in rehab was nearing an end, my wife Trish was trained to run my ventilator as well as do trach and personal care. We did a couple trial runs by spending the weekend at home to test things out. On a positive note, because of the two-thousand calorie diet they had me on, my weight increased to one hundred and ten pounds.

Besides not being able to walk anymore, which is incredible in itself. As a C5 quadriplegic, I cannot use the restroom on my own anymore. I need help with bed baths and my physical therapy. I need help to sit up in bed. To turn side-to-side. To get dressed and undressed. I am unable to get myself in and out of bed. And if your injury is higher than a C5 level, you are even more dependent on others. Basic actions are beyond your capabilities—things like scratching your own forehead, blowing your nose, brushing your teeth, or simply getting a glass of water.

If you are married, this significantly alters the dynamic of your relationship. You are essentially hooked at the hip. If you're younger and still live at home, it creates a completely different lifestyle for your parents, siblings, and even your grandparents. This is where the deeper challenges begin. This is where we win or lose. I'm talking about learning critical relationship skills based on God's Holy Word to help you overcome difficult challenges that are causing such a high divorce rate in the disabled community.

As Trish and I pulled into our driveway to unload, reality started to settle in. *Wow*, I thought, *life is going to be very different*. We were used to getting up and going to work every week. I worked in the oil field. I ran heavy equipment. I worked on the rigs drilling for oil. I hooked up pump jacks. Did plumbing. Welded. Drove dump trucks. I also enjoyed logging timber out in the middle of the woods. I had a motorcycle and a snowmobile. I loved going hunting. Camping. All of that changed in a matter of seconds.

Carol, a nurse, was brought into our home to help me with my morning care. I knew Carol and her family personally. I went to school with her children and visited their home a couple times as a kid growing up. She was always very kind. Little did I know my life was about to take a dozen more dramatic turns. First, Carol was about to share the greatest news I had ever heard—and boy did I need some good news! My attitude was pretty good, but I had no idea what I was going to do with the rest of my life. The way I saw it, I had a huge problem. I was crippled now. I couldn't get out of my own way if I had to. On top of that, my dad never taught me to be a godly man of character. I had nothing to turn to. No one to trust or to believe in. My go-to had always been a bottle of beer (which was one of the two things my dad taught me). The other was to work hard. But that all changed when I was introduced to Jesus Christ!

> 16 Therefore let us draw near with confidence to the throne of grace, so that we may receive mercy and find grace to help in time of need (Hebrews 4:16 New American Standard Bible 1995).

God gives us the ability to overcome our limitations through the Power of the Holy Spirit. After reading God's Word and asking Carol several questions, I prayed with her to repent of my sins and became a follower of Jesus Christ. I can't begin to share with you how that single prayer changed my life. Yes, I still lay there crippled, but I now had a new nature. I was born again. I was now filled with the Holy Spirit that enables us to change. I knew God Almighty personally, and He promised me in His Word that, "If I am with you, who can be against you?" Just incredible!

^{17} Therefore if anyone is in Christ, he is a new creature; the old things passed away; behold, new things have come (2 Corinthians 5:17 New American Standard Bible 1995).

When my wife and I first returned home from the hospital, we were doing well considering everything. Then one morning, about six months later, she left to visit her family a couple blocks away. Instead of returning at 1 pm as expected, I received a phone call from my mother in-law stating my wife would not be returning.

Trials in life will test what we actually believe about God, and what we don't. I for one believe a person is far better off experiencing difficult situations that expose their belief system. It's better than going through life believing you have no need for God—or believing you have a relationship with Him when in actual fact you don't.

In hindsight, I'm really not surprised by my former wife's decision to abandon our marriage. Our relationship was based on our sinful nature, and when a serious challenge presented itself, it came down like a house of cards. Looking back, we exercised very few principles in our lives, and when it really mattered the most, our marriage imploded from within. Up until my injury, the two things that held us together were sex and partying. This turned out to be a very shallow approach to life, and in the end, it only created a huge mess. Play silly games, win silly prizes. Sadly, I probably would have done the same thing to her back then, had the shoe been on the other foot.

Reluctantly, I decided to return to the hospital to get checked out and to consider my options. To my great joy, my pulmonary doctor completely weaned me off my ventilator, but I couldn't kick my trach. When I attempted to reconcile with my wife over the next few months, she rejected the idea and stated that she was seeing someone else and had no plans of getting back together with me. We were eventually divorced and, sadly, I heard through the grapevine years later that she died from breast cancer. Although she decided to end our marriage, I am very grateful for the help she gave me. She came to the hospital on and off for ten and a half months. Right before this happened, she took me to a Bible bookstore to purchase a Bible. When we returned home, we sat in our living room while she read God's Word out loud. As I listened, I got the impression this was not the first time she had read the Bible. This was not something we had ever discussed. I hope she straightened things out with the Lord, and that she is in Heaven today. She left behind a son from a prior marriage. This is where our relationships with God, family, and friends hit home.

Well, I found myself at another crossroad in life. I had to decide whether I was going to trust God or continue to live life by my own intuition. I had very little to my name that was useful to me following my injury. But that really didn't seem to matter. In an act of God's grace, as I sat alone in that hospital room, I had with me the Bible that Trish and I had just purchased, and when I opened it up, my eyes went straight to the passage below. Some people might think that was a coincidence. I believe it was God speaking directly to me. This was the first passage I ever memorized:

> [12] Not that I have already obtained it or have already become perfect, but I press on so that I may lay hold of that for which also I was laid hold of by Christ Jesus.
>
> [13] Brethren, I do not regard myself as having laid hold of it yet; but one thing I do: forgetting what lies behind and reaching forward to what lies ahead,
>
> [14] I press on toward the goal for the prize of the upward call of God in Christ Jesus (Philippians 3:12–14 New American Standard Bible 1995).

Even though I had just come to know the Lord, I had a sense of hope that I would not have to go it alone anymore—that somehow things would turn out ok. As I read God's Word, He began to speak to my heart over and over. I felt strengthened and encouraged to trust Him no matter how difficult the future appeared. The truth is, I had never sat down and read the Bible before other than the one time with my wife. Sadly, I couldn't have told you the first thing about it if my life depended on it, which it actually does!

I said my life was about to change dramatically, and it had. But God was just getting started. My pulmonary doctor recommended I meet another patient of his by the name of Jeff Jenkins. Jeff became a C3 quadriplegic when he was struck from behind by a seventeen-year-old drunk driver. This is an example that all you have to do is be in the wrong place at the wrong time and your life will never be the same. For the next seventeen years, all he could do was blink his eyes and move his head from side to side. This is a reminder that our actions have consequences. To Jeff's credit, and to God's Glory, he never became bitter. As a Christian for many years, he would soon become my mentor and best friend. God knew my greatest need was for someone to come along side me who could teach me His Word. Who could model to me his strong faith necessary to overcome seemingly impossible odds which God had already prepared him for ahead of time. Amazing grace!

Our decisions have serious consequences. Compare the quality of a person's life and impact when they respond to trials in a positive, hopeful way through faith in God Almighty verses a negative, harmful way such as turning to drugs, alcohol, anger, and bitterness. One leads to incredible opportunities to share and model your faith. The other leads to a bleak future for the person and his or her family. We all have to consider the impact of our daily decisions. Just like the drunk driver who hit Jeff from behind, some decisions have immediate consequences—others have a compounding effect over time.

When you're going through a seemingly impossible situation, always remember the example of David and Goliath in the Bible found in first Samuel chapter seventeen.

David was a shepherd boy, the youngest of eight sons. Goliath was nine feet tall. King Saul's army were all afraid of him. David, however, was filled with faith and a passion to serve and honor God, Who Goliath had blasphemed. Therefore, David slew Goliath with a sling and a stone.

David's faith was so strong that he believed with all his heart that God would go before him. That He would enable him to defeat Goliath.

^{36} Your servant has killed both the lion and the bear; and this uncircumcised Philistine will be like one of them, since he has taunted the armies of the living God." ^{37} And David said, "The Lord who delivered me from the paw of the lion and from the paw of the bear, He will deliver me from the hand of this Philistine." And Saul said to David, "Go, and may the Lord be with you." (1 Samuel 17:36–37 New American Standard Bible 1995).

David's faith was born out of the different experiences he had prior to the fight. The Lord had delivered him out of dangerous situations in the past, which proved to David that God was trustworthy and powerful.

This is another clear example of God's faithfulness. The catch is that we have to know God personally and build a relationship with Him first, then the trust follows, and the more you trust Him, the more your faith grows, and the more your faith grows, the more you will grow.

Without God's help, there is no effective way that would truly result in the kind of outcome necessary to adequately address all the difficult challenges we face. Whether you're physically crippled, or you are dealing with some other issue, learn to trust God fully and completely. Don't let your circumstances control or defeat you—see them as a path to renewal. If you are struggling mentally, emotionally, physically, or spiritually, understand that there is a way out. Our strength comes from following Christ's example. We desperately need to learn to trust God and His promises. Once again, God was faithful to His Word and took the severe tragedy that occurred in Jeff's life and turned it into good. The verse below is very comforting.

> [28] And we know that God causes all things to work together for good to those who love God, to those who are called according to His purpose (Romans 8:28 New American Standard Bible 1995).

Jeff was a huge blessing in my life and in the lives of many others. Seven years after we met, he became my best man when God sent me my precious wife Michelle. I had prayed for seven years following my divorce from my first wife. As it turned out, Michelle had been praying for seven years as well. I had put an ad in the newspaper for a caregiver. During our interview we immediately hit it off. She was a peach! Cute, too! I scheduled her for a second interview, and my older sister, Pam, said, "What? He never has second interviews."

Well, to make a long story short, I hired her, and six weeks later I asked her if she would marry me some day, thinking a year or two down the road. Well, four and a half months later we went down the aisle together with two hundred and fifty people attending our wedding. Just incredible! God is good!

Against all odds, we celebrated our twenty-seven-year anniversary on August 25, 2023. A miracle. By the grace of God, our marriage is stronger than ever before. Simply applying His Word directly to our everyday lives has made all the difference in the world. Get rid of any and all other old habits or approaches!

Without question, overcoming the challenges in our marriage—from my injury to old scars from our childhood—has been very difficult. And, we would add, the most rewarding and life changing. We give God alone all the glory and praise and thanks for everything He has done in our lives and will do moving forward. Like all marriages, it hasn't always been pretty, but we can't give up, and we didn't when we could have many times. God has always been faithful to help us overcome every challenge we've ever faced as He continues to teach us more and more every single day. It's never just about changing your circumstances that lead to greater joy in life, it's about changing your heart to see things God's way. Learn to see things in seasons.

Well, Jeff and I stayed in touch regularly until he passed away while he was recovering in the hospital from bronchitis. The evening before, he was feeling much better and excited about returning home. The following day his blood gases dropped out of sight, and he passed away early that morning. Jeff had expressed his desire to forego life support should it come to that, and in the end it did, and he went home to meet his Savior. I can see us both standing in our glorified bodies at the foot of God's throne one day soon, as we praise and thank Him for everything He so graciously did to bless our lives!

The hope and excitement for every Christian is the promise of Heaven.

[3] If I go and prepare a place for you, I will come again and receive you to Myself, that where I am, there you may be also (John 14:3 New American Standard Bible 1995).

The word Heaven is mentioned two-hundred-and-seventy-six times in the New Testament alone. There will be no more separation because death will be conquered. We will be celebrating our Lord and Savior Jesus Christ every single day. Just incredible! I wonder who will lead praise and worship? Totally off the charts! Imagine being in the presence of God for all eternity. To be loved and cared for perfectly. The fellowship between us all will be just incredible. Imagine everyone loving each other in a pure and holy way every day, all day, *forever and ever!*

Imagine never experiencing any hurt, pain, or fear of any kind ever again. There won't be any health issues, cares, or concerns. We will all have an eternal glorified body that will last forever. No more pain pills. No more illnesses whatsoever. We will have true freedom that will never be taken away. Joy inexpressible, peace everlasting. Beauty beyond description. Your mortgage in Heaven has been paid in full thanks to Jesus Christ who died on the Cross for all our sins. Never forget that! Heaven will be way beyond what we've always longed for and could ever imagine. We will all love each other unconditionally. How precious is that? We will rule and reign with God Almighty forever and ever. Get ready!

> [4] and He will wipe away every tear from their eyes; and there will no longer be any death; there will no longer be any mourning, or crying, or pain; the first things have passed away." (Revelation 21:4 New American Standard Bible).

I thank God for Jeff's life and Christlike example. He learned to live far beyond his circumstances. One thing he said to me that I will never forget was, "Lawrence, this is the first day of the rest of your life." That spoke volumes to me. Every day is an opportunity to start over and change the path you're on. When life gets off track—and it will—we just need to have the wisdom and discernment to make the necessary corrections. And as long as our decisions are based on God's Word, we will have peace. My wife Michelle and I have a couple signs in our bedroom. One says, "Live life today, yesterday is gone, and tomorrow may never come." The other one says, "Speak softly, Love tenderly, Pray fervently."

> [3] Blessed be the God and Father of our Lord Jesus Christ, the Father of mercies and God of all comfort, [4] who comforts us in all our affliction so that we will be able to comfort those who are in any affliction with the comfort with which we ourselves are comforted by God (2 Corinthians 1:3–4).

The hope of Heaven is only hopeful if it is based on God's Holy Word. I'm reminded of a gravestone in my hometown that reads, "Dear friends, remember me as you pass by, as you are now, so once was I. Youth and bloom were my pride, that now is laid aside. As I am now so you will be, prepare for death and follow me."

That poem caught my attention as a youth.

Some believe the only thing certain in life is death and taxes. If this person had any kind of hope in the afterlife, he didn't express it here. He just invited people to follow him. But follow him too where? What is your hope based on today when you slip into eternity? Have you come up with a sound decision that has given you true peace, knowing that if your heart stopped tonight, your soul would enter heaven? I have talked to many people who act like it's no big deal. They *act* like they are not concerned. Does anybody really believe when a person is sentenced to prison for life that he or she is excited about it? People are being deceived. Satan is having a field day. Instead of believing God, they are believing Satan's lies because it feeds their sinful nature. This illustrates the effects of sin in our lives, and the ability of Satan to deceive us. This dichotomy of sin and life is summed up well in Romans 8:

> [6] For the mind set on the flesh is death, but the mind set on the Spirit is life and peace, [7] because the mind set on the flesh is hostile toward God; for it does not subject itself to the law of God, for it is not even able to do so, [8] and those who are in the flesh cannot please God.
>
> [9] However, you are not in the flesh but in the Spirit, if indeed the Spirit of

God dwells in you. But if anyone does not have the Spirit of Christ, he does not belong to Him. [10] If Christ is in you, though the body is dead because of sin, yet the spirit is alive because of righteousness. [11] But if the Spirit of Him who raised Jesus from the dead dwells in you, He who raised Christ Jesus from the dead will also give life to your mortal bodies through His Spirit who dwells in you (Romans 8:6–11 New American Standard Bible 1995).

If you had a life-threatening illness, wouldn't you research the topic like no tomorrow? Would you not find out all you could on the subject to give yourself some kind of hope? Yet, in a similar way, what have you done to research history? If we are being honest with ourselves, we all have a life-threatening disease and there is only one cure. The illness is sin, and unless we are washed in the blood of the Lamb, it will never go away.

We know Jesus is the Messiah and the only begotten Son of God because of Bible prophesies He fulfilled. Open up a Bible and ask God to speak to your heart. He is faithful to His Word. Believe and be healed. Believe and be transformed. Get busy fulfilling your ministry for God's Glory while you still have an opportunity in this life.

The more you read God's Word, the more your faith will grow. The more your confidence will grow. Not in yourself, but in Him. Then you will start singing beautiful praise and worship songs to thank Him for all the precious promises found in His Holy Word as it totally transforms your entire life. Just incredible!

Pray for wisdom daily. Satan and his demons are constantly at work to discourage us at every turn. *This is very serious!* Get wise to the devil and how he operates. Be intentional with sharing the Good News with your family, friends, and neighbors. Satan divides our families in an effort to destroy society. Deception, division, destruction. We have stopped applying God's Word to our lives in the way that we need to. We have all gone astray. It's time for each of us to take up our cross and follow Christ's example!

Think about how divided our families have become. When was the last time you lost a loved one, for example? Were you in good standing with them, or did you really struggle through the grieving process because of missed opportunities? It's never easy losing someone, but the sorrow we experience is compounded greatly when there is distance between us and them, and we stay stuck there, sometimes for the rest of our lives. This is not healthy for anyone. This can be fixed by cutting out the things in your life that are not nearly as important.

We have all been deceived by the enemy who is out to destroy our lives. We all have to rethink our position as we move forward. We have to get back to the Word of God! Back to going to church! Submit and obey, starting today!

God has designed the family to function beautifully and wonderfully. Parenting is a golden opportunity to pass your faith on to the next generation and the devil knows that. Therefore, he is doing everything he can to stop you. Just look at all the attacks on parents and precious innocent children all around the world. God created each beloved child in His image. Because of evil rotten sin, impressionable children are being exploited today in unimaginable ways.

> [20] Woe to those who call evil good, and good evil (Isaiah 5:20 New American Standard Bible 1995).

> [2] It would be better for him if a millstone were hung around his neck and he were thrown into the sea, than that he would cause one of these little ones to stumble (Luke 17:2 New American Standard Bible 1995).

Trust is the key to all relationships. Without it, there is no relationship. When a child carries distrust into their adult life, they will naturally struggle to connect with God and others. Just take a minute to recall your own childhood and how that may be affecting you as an adult today. And if you have a family of your own, consider how things could unfold a decade or two from now. Also, consider the horrific impact on children when a parent or parents are hooked on drugs or alcohol or both. You can hear the child say to themselves, "Dad does it, Mom does it. It must be ok." That is modeling failure to them. How is that helping them to become healthy mature adults? How is that helping them to prepare for all the challenges they will certainly face in this life?

Divorce is another experience children are forced to deal with. It naturally affects the overall wellbeing of a child. They can become depressed and stay stuck there. That's when kids will take up alcohol and drugs to numb the pain. That's when they seek attention in all the wrong places. That can lead to fornication and potential pregnancy, which could possibly lead to an abortion. The taking of an innocent life. Children then tend to shake their fist at God and say, "Why did you allow this to happen to me?" when it wasn't God's doing at all.

We all need heart surgery. Instead of giving up on our marriages, we need to give up our dysfunctional lifestyles and focus on healing the relationship. Rather than getting rid of your spouse, get rid of all the unnecessary baggage in your life. Marriage is like a two-seater bike. You have to be moving in the same direction. Prayer is the most powerful life changing way to partner with your spouse. Turn your unproductive conversations into faithful prayers and watch what God will do! Begin from a position of victory! Press on and keep pressing on for God's Glory and Honor! Some of the most beautiful rainbows come after the ugliest of storms.

> [7] You husbands in the same way, live with your wives in an understanding way, as with someone weaker, since she is a woman; and show her honor as a fellow heir of the grace of life, so that your prayers will not be hindered (1 Peter 3:7 New American Standard Bible 1995).

Remember, more things are caught than taught. So, a key element that must be understood is that "if" your spouse isn't all-in at this point, you can still apply the Word of God to yourself personally, and you will change the dynamic of your marriage. By doing so, you will be able to model Christ to your spouse, which will speak to their heart.

> [6] And without faith it is impossible to

please Him, for he who comes to God must believe that He is and that He is a rewarder of those who seek Him (Hebrews 11: 6 New American Standard Bible 1995).

It's been said, "Be the person today that you want your child to grow up to be tomorrow." A parent's Christlike example of what a marriage should be like is absolutely huge! Along with effective biblical premarital advice ahead of time. This is essential to a son or daughter's future, as well as their children's wellbeing. Everyone wants their children to be successful. Wisdom from the lessons you've learned in addition to other wise counsel makes all the difference in the world. Grandparents play a vital role as they share what they've learned over the years. We used to call these traits family values. Have a look at the verse below.

> [6] Train up a child in the way he should go,
> Even when he is old he will not depart from it (Proverbs 22:6 New American Standard Bible 1995).

My parents didn't discuss these issues with me or my siblings when we were growing up. I'm not saying it's easy. Parenting is one of the greatest challenges in life. That's why we all need God's help! This isn't the kind of stuff you learn in school either. It has to be passed down, or you run the risk that your children will not have learned it until after the fact. Then just when they thought the next chapter of their life was beginning, and they go down the aisle in marriage, they soon begin to have problems they were not prepared for. And if they have begun a family of their own, it compounds the challenges they now face, and the newly born children begin to feel the impact as well.

The best thing you can possibly do is share the Good News (the Gospel) with everyone! If you are not born again, start today by coming to faith in Christ yourself. If you are a Christian and you need to recommit your life to Christ, pray now and get moving forward again. And if you have been steadily walking with the Lord, be very intentional to take your walk to the next level and beyond—from glory-to-glory in Christlikeness. Share the Gospel with your children as you continually pour into their lives. Glory to His name! God has a beautiful plan for all of our lives. Don't settle for second or third place. Repent, and get rid of any and all sin in your life. Tell Satan to jump in the lake. Get focused on completing the plans God has for your life!

[33] But seek first His kingdom and His

righteousness, and all these things will be added to you (Matthew 6:33 New American Standard Bible 1995).

Life is like a spiritual exam every day. Every opportunity we have is precious. Time is not on our side! The hour is late, and the clock is ticking.

Our Salvation comes by faith alone, in Christ alone. All our righteous deeds are tainted by sin and are not acceptable to warrant our Salvation. Think of your sin as a legal debt, and because of it, we are all under legal judgement from God. And the judgement for breaking the law is death and eternal separation from God unless we become born again.

> [23] For the wages of sin is death, but the free gift of God is eternal life in Christ Jesus our Lord (Romans 6:23 New American Standard Bible 1995).

God's Righteousness is the standard. There is only love in the heart of God! He is Holy and Righteous, and we are not. We are incapable of such a standard because of the effects of our sinful nature, thus the need for the forgiveness of our sins through the incarnation of Jesus who is God in the flesh.

> [1] In the beginning was the Word,

and the Word was with God, and the
Word was God (John 1:1 New American
Standard Bible 1995).

¹⁴ And the Word became flesh, and
dwelt among us, and we saw His glory,
glory as of the only begotten from the
Father, full of grace and truth (John 1:14
New American Standard Bible 1995).

Jesus cancelled our sin debt when He bore our sin
on the Cross. We just have to exercise our faith
and believe in the One True God for our Salvation!
Absolutely incredible!

⁶ For a child will be born to us, a son will
be given to us;
And the government will rest on His
shoulders;
And His name will be called Wonderful
Counselor, Mighty God,
Eternal Father, Prince of Peace (Isaiah
9:6 New American Standard Bible
1995).

¹⁶ "For God so loved the world, that
He gave His only begotten Son, that
whoever believes in Him shall not
perish, but have eternal life (John 3:16
New American Standard Bible 1995).

[5] For there is one God, and one mediator also between God and men, the man Christ Jesus (1 Timothy 2:5 New American Standard Bible 1995).

[10] let it be known to all of you and to all the people of Israel, that by the name of Jesus Christ the Nazarene, whom you crucified, whom God raised from the dead—by this name this man stands here before you in good health. [11] He is the stone which was rejected by you, the builders, but which became the chief corner stone. [12] And there is salvation in no one else; for there is no other name under heaven that has been given among men by which we must be saved." (Acts 4:10–12 New American Standard Bible).

[20] I have been crucified with Christ; and it is no longer I who live, but Christ lives in me; and the life which I now live in the flesh I live by faith in the Son of God, who loved me and gave Himself up for me (Galatians 2:20 New American Standard Bible 1995).

There is a big difference between a relationship and religion. Religion is a belief in a god or in many gods. It's an organized system of ceremonies and rules that a group of people observe. God, on the other hand, created mankind to have a family. To enjoy a personal relationship with us, and us with Him. After the fall of mankind, Jesus died on the Cross for our sins to redeem us back into His Kingdom as His children to love and to care for us. When we enter into a personal relationship with our Heavenly Father, we become followers, disciples, and ambassadors for Christ. There is not a more pure, intimate, loving, caring, giving relationship in all the world. As followers of Jesus Christ, like the disciples in the New Testament, we are not here to convert people to a religion. Our calling is to introduce a sinful, falling, lost, and hurting world to Jesus Christ by sharing the Gospel with them. Thus, starting a relationship with Him. Not some form of a man-made religion designed to accommodate man's sins. This is clearly another way Satan has manipulated the truth. Carefully consider the passages below.

> [1] But the Spirit explicitly says that in later times some will fall away from the faith, paying attention to deceitful spirits and doctrines of demons (1

Timothy 4:1 New American Standard Bible 1995).

⁴ For certain persons have crept in unnoticed, those who were long beforehand marked out for this condemnation, ungodly persons who turn the grace of our God into licentiousness and deny our only Master and Lord, Jesus Christ (Jude 1:4 New American Standard Bible 1995).

¹³ For such men are false apostles, deceitful workers, disguising themselves as apostles of Christ. ¹⁴ No wonder, for even Satan disguises himself as an angel of light. ¹⁵ Therefore it is not surprising if his servants also disguise themselves as servants of righteousness, whose end will be according to their deeds (2 Corinthians 11:13–15 New American Standard Bible 1995).

Purgatory is another example of how Satan deceives people in an effort to undermine God's truth. You might recall when Christ was on the Cross and He said to the one thief that believed, "Today you shall be with Me in paradise." He did not have any time to do good works. Some people misunderstand the commands about doing good deeds in the Bible. Doing good deeds is the result of a person's Salvation, not the basis of it. We are saved for good works, *not by good works.*

> [43] And He said to him, "Truly I say to you, today you shall be with Me in Paradise." (Luke 23:43 New American Standard Bible 1995).

> [8] We are of good courage, I say, and prefer rather to be absent from the body and to be at home with the Lord (2 Corinthians 5:8 New American Standard Bible 1995).

> [10] For we are His workmanship, created in Christ Jesus for good works, which God prepared beforehand so that we would walk in them (Ephesians 2:10 New American Standard Bible 1995).

> [8] Therefore do not be ashamed of the testimony of our Lord or of me His prisoner, but join with me in suffering for the gospel according to the power of God, [9] who has saved us and called us with a holy calling, not according to

our works, but according to His own purpose and grace which was granted us in Christ Jesus from all eternity (2 Timonthy 1:8–9 New American Standard Bible 1995).

Don't confuse faith as a work, it is not. It is God Himself who is at work in our lives. He initiated everything. For God so loved the world that He gave His only begotten Son. God loves us perfectly, and because of that, He left Heaven temporarily to come done here to die for our sins to redeem us back into His Holy Kingdom. That is good news for all of us!

> [2] fixing our eyes on Jesus, the author and perfecter of faith, who for the joy set before Him endured the cross, despising the shame, and has sat down at the right hand of the throne of God (Hebrews 12:2 New American Standard Bible 1995).

Pray in faith at every turn. Our Lord and Savior is listening, and He obviously cares and desires deeply to help us in every way! Humble yourself before it's too late!

CHAPTER SEVEN: RESPONDING TO LIFE'S CIRCUMSTANCES

[7] Do not be deceived, God is not mocked; for whatever a man sows, this he will also reap. [8] For the one who sows to his own flesh will from the flesh reap corruption, but the one who sows to the Spirit will from the Spirit reap eternal life. [9] Let us not lose heart in doing good, for in due time we will reap if we do not grow weary. [10] So then, while we have opportunity, let us do good to all people, and especially to those who are of the household of the faith (Galatians 6:7–10 New American Standard Bible).

There are a few questions every Christian must answer. Where exactly do you stand with God today? What exactly is taking place in your life that is pleasing or displeasing to Him? When you fall short, are you determined to correct it and live a more Christlike life based on God's Word? Are you being intentional to fulfill your ministry as a servant of God for His Glory and Praise, or are you still being deceived by Satan's lies and deceptions?

> [12] Therefore I urge you, brethren, by the mercies of God, to present your bodies a living and holy sacrifice, acceptable to God, which is your spiritual service of worship (Romans 12:1 New American Standard Bible 1995).

> [1] Therefore, since we have so great a cloud of witnesses surrounding us, let us also lay aside every encumbrance and the sin which so easily entangles us, and let us run with endurance the race that is set before us, [2] fixing our eyes on Jesus, the author and perfecter of faith, who for the joy set before Him endured the cross, despising the shame, and has sat down at the right hand of the throne of God (Hebrews 12:1–2 New American Standard Bible 1995).

Depending on which direction your life is heading, you may need to reconsider your lifestyle. Does it match Christ's example to us, or are you doing your own thing? Are your circumstances self-inflicted, manmade, natural, or by design? Maybe it's a relationship that you're involved in that is less than God's best?

> [1] How blessed is the man who does not walk in the counsel of the wicked,
> Nor stand in the path of sinners,
> Nor sit in the seat of scoffers!
>
> [2] But his delight is in the law of the Lord, And in His law he meditates day and night.
>
> [3] He will be like a tree firmly planted by streams of water,
> Which yields its fruit in its season
> And its leaf does not wither;
> And in whatever he does, he prospers (Psalm 1:1–3 New American Standard Bible 1995).

These are the hard questions that most people don't like to answer. This usually means they are content with living life any way they choose. A person's life has the potential to change when their circumstances reveal the consequences of their choices. Where exactly do you stand with God today? This is a critical element of any trial you're going through and must be thoroughly considered when facing questions that deal with important matters. *To do otherwise, you are choosing to eliminate the most significant aspect of all of life, and that is God Himself.*

When was the last time you really thought about God and how you factor into His Kingdom? Have you seriously taken the time necessary to reflect on where you stand with Him? What did you conclude? Be honest. Is He a welcomed presence in your life, or do you wish He would just go away?

Mankind has achieved great things in many ways, but technology isn't going to save you. At the same time, man has done unimaginable evil. For one, how do you slaughter an innocent, defenseless baby and try to justify it? We kill our own and think nothing of it, and then go to great lengths to defend it. This is not going to end well!

> [20] Woe to those who call evil good, and good evil (Isaiah 5:20 New American Standard Bible 1995).

If sin sounds like the resounding theme here, that's because it is until it's exchanged for Christ's shed blood on the Cross. Maybe you are like I was and believed God is real but didn't understand that we are separated from Him because of our sinful nature. Once I came to this realization, I had no problem believing it. The truth is we all have a problem called sin, and it's time to be honest about it and act.

Today my wife Michelle and I enjoy a

wonderful, intimate relationship with God that we wouldn't trade for anything in the world. We are amazed by God's Word and all His teaching that is specifically designed to help us, and we only understand a tiny bit in comparison to what we have yet to learn. Until our eyes are opened by God, we will continue to struggle because manmade solutions only address our superficial problems. And not the deep-seated crisis which is our separation from God because of our sin, and how that affects every single thing in our lives.

This is a God-size problem that we cannot fix outside of His design to redeem mankind back into His Kingdom. And the trials you are currently facing are your ticket to a new life through Jesus Christ. It's important to realize there are different kinds of healing. But the most important one of all is a spiritual healing between us and God. The thing to remember is there are always lessons we can learn in life. But because we often miss them, God puts us through trials so that we are forced to reconsider our ways. Sometimes our problems are small and easy to figure out, and other times they are much more complex.

As we learn to trust and obey God, we put the onus on Him. We cannot fix ourselves. By trusting Him for the answers, this changes the way we function in the midst of our trials. When we come to realize how dependent we are on God, we enter into the freedom that is provided to us through the Cross. When we focus our attention on the person of Jesus Christ and surrender our lives over to that which pleases Him, we begin to see life from a completely different perspective.

Learning to accept trials as a method that God uses to transform our hearts and minds is a critical step in our maturity as Christians. It does us no good to get rattled and lose our peace over and over when different things happen in our lives. You either believe that God is in control, or you don't. Learning to apply God's grace to every situation and looking to Him to help us discern the lesson He desires to teach us is far greater than any other alternative.

When we get triggered and allow our circumstances to control us, we forfeit the working power of the Holy Spirit. By learning to communicate with God through prayer by faith, you can manage your life without forfeiting control to someone other than the Holy Spirit. As a Christian, when we acknowledge Christ as Lord, we have surrendered our lives to Him, and we now belong to Him to do as He wills, which is to transform us into His Holy likeness, so that we are without sin. This empowers us to overcome anything in life.

The thing about overreacting to something that has already happened is- you can't put the milk back into the bottle. And now that it's out, you have to decide how to best respond in a way that recognizes God and His promises first and foremost. Overreacting doesn't change what just happened, it only keeps you stuck on first base.

Naturally if your situation is much more severe, there may be a grieving process as you adjust to changes. As you grieve, the one thing that will help you regulate the changes you're going through is a genuine faith that generates trust in God—no matter how difficult things appear. This is not easy at first because it's opposite of what we are used to doing. Fear is a powerful force. It's one of Satan's favorite tools and biggest schemes. But if you can maintain a solid biblical perspective, it will help you manage all the emotional ups and downs of life in a peaceful manner.

When your life gets tipped upside down, it's helpful to look back to your childhood to see how the experiences of your youth may have affected you and your perspective on life now as an adult. It will also help you to examine your parents' childhood and adult life (as well as your grandparents' life, if possible) to discern what their character was like.

The process may be uncomfortable but be strong and dare to pull back the curtain and take an honest look. You just might be surprised to find some answers to questions you've been wondering about for some time. Things get passed down, both good and bad, and it is each generation's responsibility to improve upon the last. When something happened at home as a child, how did your parents manage it? Then ask yourself, how could those experiences be affecting me today as an individual, a spouse, a parent, or as a neighbor?

We've all heard the expression, "We are a product of our childhood." When we leave home, these traits go with us and have an impact on all our relationships—including how we view God. When we were growing up as children, we formed sinful habits by filling our minds with immoral thoughts through television, the internet, and other experiences. And when we began to entertain some of them, or act them out, they ended up becoming a part of us. Sometimes this is a subtle thing that gradually happens over time. As these changes occur in our lives, we are being conditioned to accept them as normal behavior. And in a world that is encouraging this everywhere today, many people are being greatly deceived.

When you get older and realize the negative effects these experiences have had on your life, you begin to look for answers. As you attempt to correct these things in your life, you begin to realize it is impossible without God's help. As we each attempt to correct the problems and separate ourselves from these destructive behavioral patterns, we must first be honest about any sin in our lives, and deal with it in a biblical manner.

Consequently, the conflict and strife that revolves around our lives as a result of this come in different forms. There are some trials that will rob you of all hope if you let it. As the saying goes, "Don't make long-term decisions during short-term circumstances." This is why the divorce rate is so high. Or why some people decide to abort a precious little child. Or to end their life by committing suicide. This is all very tragic, and it is tearing our families and society apart! This is Satan at his best. He slips untruths into our heads, and if we are not wise to his lies and deceptions, away we go down the wrong road.

As Christians, we have all acted out of our flesh and grieved our Lord on many occasions. None of us initially enjoy those times when we're forced to face the truth simply because we don't relish looking behind the curtain. Again, like Adam and Eve, we initially try to hide behind fig leaves and attempt to avoid responsibility. If we're being honest with ourselves, we would rather pretend and keep all our dirty laundry out of sight and out of mind. Exactly where Satan wants it to stay. The best thing we can do is get wise to how he operates against us to keep us stuck where we are at, which is the complete opposite of what God would have us do! Who do you believe has your best interest at hand, God or Satan?

Change is very difficult, and it takes a lot of willingness and effort on our part. It also takes a frank and honest discussion with everyone involved. If you are married, for example, it will mean twice the effort as you transform two different personalities, backgrounds, and experiences into one. That is why if you are a Christian, you marry a Christian, so you don't end up with two completely different opposing world views.

> ^{14} Do not be bound together with unbelievers; for what partnership have righteousness and lawlessness, or what fellowship has light with darkness? (2 Corinthians 6:14 New American Standard Bible 1995).

> ^{17} But He knew their thoughts and said to them, "Any kingdom divided against itself is laid waste; and a house divided against itself falls (Luke 11:17 New American Standard Bible 1995).

Trying to live life without God is like being stranded on a raft in the middle of the Pacific Ocean during a horrific storm. Maybe you haven't experienced a storm of this magnitude yet. Or maybe you have just received a warning that you need to get prepared for things to come. Perhaps you have seen the storm coming for some time and you're bracing for landfall. Either way you look at it, storms are inevitable, and they affect us all. The reality is, if you have never repented of your sin and began to follow Jesus Christ as your Savior and Lord, you need to get serious about it today.

Truth requires us to look at ourselves in the mirror and have a moment of honesty before God. When you think of it, who are we really kidding, anyway? People who know us best are aware of our shortcomings and we are aware of theirs. Don't be fooled. God is keeping track of every little detail of your life.

Sooner or later, we come to realize we're not happy with the way things are going—that the deceptive dream the world calls success hasn't worked out. Along the way you thought it was just going to cost you a little extra here and there. Instead, it has slowly undermined your life, including your marriage, and your relationship with your children. What good is a million dollars in the bank at the expense of your family?

God is gracious to us, and learning to trust Him is the only way to go through life. This is the first step to a life of freedom. God is not the bad guy here as some try to make Him out to be. Sin is a problem we all must face in our lives. All God has done is offer the only solution to the problem, and that is His Son's death as a bridge between our sin and a Holy and Righteous God.

I believe we all start out trying to live life the best way we know how. And that is what has led you to where you are today. The problem is we've lost our way, and we don't bother to read the manual until all else fails. I remember the day I was injured. I thought I was just minding my own business. Like the Apostle Paul, I had my own agenda, and it didn't include God. Fortunately for me, like the Apostle Paul, God had a different plan. And in a similar way that God directed Ananias to come to Paul to open his eyes, Carol, my nurse, followed God's command and shared the Gospel with me. The truth is we all desperately need God's help, and we know it. The problem is we've come to believe our own rhetoric and the rhetoric of others and have forgotten who is the potter, and who is the clay.

Suffering can be described as anything causing pain or distress. Affliction became a part of our lives with the entrance of sin into the world, and because of it, misery is a common human experience. It is impossible for us to avoid natural calamity, physical injury, and interpersonal conflict. But like I said, following the Fall of mankind, God causes or allows these things to happen in our lives for a reason, and that is to draw us to Himself so we can experience amazing healing and transformation. I see it as an act of God's grace!

Adam and Eve were created in God's image and enjoyed a perfect and Holy existence, completely fulfilled in their fellowship with Him. That was until they disobeyed God and believed Satan's lie. As a result, mankind was cursed. This is when our troubles began, and we have experienced the effects of this *spiritual* death ever since. This explains our eventual physical death that we will each experience, which explains all the suffering we go through in this life. This is a reality that every human being must decide for themselves, and it depends on your perspective on God Almighty.

Do you realize you only have two choices? Either you believe in the Creation account described in Genesis, chapter one, or you have placed your faith for your future in evolution. Yes, you have the free will to decide how you want to live your life. But what if you knew God loved you so much that He died in your place to pay the penalty for your sin? He did this in order for you to come to know Him personally as your Heavenly Father and enter His Kingdom for all eternity. Talk about amazing grace!

Most people struggle with the concept of God because they don't understand how God could allow pain and suffering. I believe that's because of a worldview that doesn't match that of

Scripture. With a correct biblical perspective, life begins to make much more sense, and suffering becomes easier to manage if we understand why it's happening and learn to unleash its potential.

One of the first things we need to do is view the world the same way God does. And that is described in detail for us throughout the Word of God. Truthfully, we make things much harder for ourselves than they have to be. We hesitate to act because we are ashamed or uncomfortable with opening up our lives to others, which is natural at first. But when you come to realize Satan puts these thoughts in our head as a way to discourage us from starting a precious relationship with God, then we need to quickly recognize it for what it is and do the right thing.

If you have a problem, you can't fix it unless you follow the repair manual. And until we decide to follow the directions written in the Word of God, we will continue in our sin. In my life, it was my accident that snapped me out of the delusion I was living in. I never tire of thanking God for all He has done in my life by opening my eyes to see His Glory and experience Him personally every single day. You won't either, I promise.

Life is a personal journey that we are all on. Accountability to God is an individual responsibility. So, do the right thing today and ask Him for the forgiveness of your sins, and start over.

CHAPTER EIGHT: THE FALL OF MANKIND

As a result of Adam and Eve's disobedience to the revealed will of God, man's eyes were opened to sin. Adam and Eve were escorted out of the Garden of Eden and God's Holy presence. God then cursed Satan, the earth, and mankind, and we now live in a sinful, fallen, and cursed world. The book of Genesis sums up this decline:

> [9] Then the Lord God called to the man, and said to him, "Where are you?" [10] He said, "I heard the sound of You in the garden, and I was afraid because I was naked; so I hid myself." [11] And He said, "Who told you that you were naked? Have you eaten from the tree of which I commanded you not to eat?" [12] The man said, "The woman whom You gave to be with me, she gave me from the tree, and I ate." [13] Then the Lord God said to the woman, "What is this you

have done?" And the woman said, "The serpent deceived me, and I ate." ^{14} The Lord God said to the serpent, "Because you have done this, cursed are you more than all cattle,
and more than every beast of the field; on your belly you will go, and dust you will eat

all the days of your life; ^{15} And I will put enmity between you and the woman,
and between your seed and her seed; he shall bruise you on the head, and you

shall bruise him on the heel." ^{16} To the woman He said, "I will greatly multiply your pain in childbirth.
In pain you will bring forth children; yet your desire will be for your husband,

and he will rule over you." ^{17} Then to Adam He said, "Because you have listened to the voice of your wife, and have eaten from the tree about which I commanded you, saying, 'You shall not eat from it'; cursed is the ground because of you; in toil you will eat of it

all the days of your life. ^{18} "Both thorns and thistles it shall grow for you; and you will eat the plants of the field;

^{19} By the sweat of your face you will

eat bread, till you return to the ground, because from it you were taken; for you are dust, and to dust you shall return." (Genesis 3:9–19 New American Standard Bible 1995).

Notice in verse thirteen, when Eve responds to God's question, she says, "The serpent deceived me, and I ate." Satan has been deceiving us all ever since. It's crucial that we take this seriously. How do we win the spiritual battle we're in as Christians if we ignore the fact that Satan is set on destroying our lives? In order to be in God's presence in Heaven, we must be born again. To make this possible, Jesus Christ died on the Cross for man's sins and rose from the grave three days later. In doing so, Jesus defeated Satan, death, hell, and the grave, making mankind's redemption possible. Because of the fallen, sinful nature that we are born with through the loins of Adam, we no longer naturally desire to live a righteous life. We have all sinned greatly against a Holy God, beginning at birth, and will be held accountable. If you doubt this, refer to Ephesians 2. It describes a person's life prior to coming to Christ:

> [1] And you were dead in your trespasses and sins, [2] in which you formerly walked according to the course of this

world, according to the prince of the power of the air, of the spirit that is now working in the sons of disobedience. [3] Among them we too all formerly lived in the lusts of our flesh, indulging the desires of the flesh and of the mind, and were by nature children of wrath, even as the rest (Ephesians 2:1–3 New American Standard Bible 1995).

How do you view sin in your life, and what are you doing about it? Like I said, some people have no problem with sin and think nothing of it. They continue living a sinful lifestyle like it's acceptable when it clearly is not. Before I got saved, I would sin and not really care because it was my nature to do so, but that doesn't make it right. Then there are other people who, because of the message of the Gospel, are convicted by their sin and repent.

[9] The Lord is not slow about His promise, as some count slowness, but is patient toward you, not wishing for any to perish but for all to come to repentance (2 Peter 3:9 New American Standard Bible 1995).

As a kid, I grew up in the grape belt in western New York, and from the time I was little, I worked in the vineyards. As I grew older, I learned to trim grapes in the fall and winter months. We pruned away all the dead wood from the vine, creating new growth that produced a fruitful harvest at the end of summer.

Abiding in the vine can be achieved only by fully submitting to God. This leads to a triumphant lifestyle over your past, present, and future. Up until now, you may have been trying to do things in your own strength. This will never work simply because it's not God's design for man's redemption and sanctification. As stated in John 15:

[1] "I am the true vine, and My Father is the vinedresser. [2] Every branch in Me that does not bear fruit, He takes away; and every branch that bears fruit, He prunes it so that it may bear more fruit. [3] You are already clean because of the word which I have spoken to you. [4] Abide in Me, and I in you. As the branch cannot bear fruit of itself unless it abides in the vine, so neither can you unless you abide in Me. [5] I am the vine, you are the branches; he who abides in Me and I in him, he bears much fruit, for apart from Me you can do nothing. [6]

If anyone does not abide in Me, he is thrown away as a branch and dries up; and they gather them, and cast them into the fire and they are burned. [7] If you abide in Me, and My words abide in you, ask whatever you wish, and it will be done for you. [8] My Father is glorified by this, that you bear much fruit, and so prove to be My disciples. [9] Just as the Father has loved Me, I have also loved you; abide in My love. [10] If you keep My commandments, you will abide in My love; just as I have kept My Father's commandments and abide in His love. [11] These things I have spoken to you so that My joy may be in you, and that your joy may be made full (John 15: 1–11 New American Standard Bible 1995).

These verses remind us of the hope that every believer can enjoy every day. Notice that the branch cannot bear fruit unless it abides in the vine. The pruning process begins as God separates His children from their sinful nature. Again, this is known as the old man, and the things of this world that are designed to deceive and destroy us.

²² that, in reference to your former manner of life, you lay aside the old self, which is being corrupted in accordance with the lusts of deceit, ²³ and that you be renewed in the spirit of your mind, ²⁴ and put on the new self, which in the likeness of God has been created in righteousness and holiness of the truth (Ephesians 4:22–24 New American Standard Bible 1995).

The Apostle Paul reminds us of the battle we go through as Christians when he said, "For what I am doing, I do not understand; for I am not practicing what I would like to do, but I am doing the very thing I hate." (Romans 7:15 New American Standard Bible 1995). This describes every Christian's life; the ongoing battle between obeying Christ and being deceived by Satan and acting out of our flesh.

Notice how Adam and Eve tried to pass the blame to someone other than themselves. Adam passed the blame to Eve when he said, "The woman that You gave me, she gave me fruit of the tree and I ate." And Eve passed the blame when she said, "The Serpent deceived me, and I ate."

Yes, Eve was deceived by Satan, but she had a free will to decide for herself, just like Adam did, and in the same way you and I do today. We all do the same thing when we fail to take responsibility for our actions, and we blame our problems on our parents, spouses, friends, the weather—anyone but ourselves. As long as we continue to make excuses, we will remain in our current state that may have you separated from God because of unforgiven sin. And if you are a Christian, maybe you need to examine your spiritual walk with our Lord to determine what He is trying to say to you through this present season of your life.

The first step is to take ownership of any and all sin in your life. This is a spiritual exercise that takes a believer to new heights in their walk with God, and the more we are challenged, the stronger our faith can become. Consider the following passages from James 1 and 2 Corinthians carefully:

> [2] Consider it all joy, my brethren, when you encounter various trials, [3] knowing that the testing of your faith produces endurance. [4] And let endurance have its perfect result, so that you may be perfect and complete, lacking in nothing.
>
> [5] But if any of you lacks wisdom, let him ask of God, who gives to all generously and without reproach, and it

will be given to him (James 1:2–5 New American Standard Bible 1995).

⁹ And He has said to me, "My grace is sufficient for you, for power is perfected in weakness." Most gladly, therefore, I will rather boast about my weaknesses, so that the power of Christ may dwell in me.

¹⁰ Therefore I am well content with weaknesses, with insults, with distresses, with persecutions, with difficulties, for Christ's sake; for when I am weak, then I am strong (2 Corinthians 12:9–10 New American Standard Bible 1995).

One of the beautiful things about a relationship with God is that He never changes. We can faithfully submit to His will because God is Holy. And we can completely trust that He has our absolute best interest in mind because it is completely against His nature to do otherwise. Therefore, we can fully trust Him in all things and at all times.

This means that once a person becomes a born-again Christian, they can confidently place their trust in God to provide the wisdom and humility necessary to persevere through difficult times. This is the key to keeping your joy intact and having peace no matter what your circumstances may be.

The fact that God is Holy should tell us we never have to question His motives. This is incredibly liberating when you apply it correctly. Just a basic understanding of God's Sovereignty helps us know that He is in control of everything. That means He causes or allows things to happen that directly affects our lives in a personal way. Therefore, it is you and I who need to adjust to our circumstances in faith from the standpoint that the situation we find ourselves in is perfect for what God wants us to learn. We just have to respond in faith and trust Him fully and completely.

The central themes of a relationship with God are to glorify Him, praise Him, thank Him, serve Him, enjoy His Holy presence, do His Will, and achieve the purpose and plans He has for your life. God does this by opening our eyes to see His Glory, and as He draws us to Himself, we learn to trust Him completely with our very lives.

You can't be of any use to God until you start living like Him. This is a lifelong transformation that begins with a new birth into God's family. Then, through our obedience, we bear the fruit of righteousness which creates a pure heart within the new believer that God works through to reach others. You must realize that you are unique to God. He created us specifically with a purpose in mind that is far greater than our feeble attempts at life without Him.

When we embrace the idea that our greatest purpose in life is to glorify God, and we do that by completely surrendering our lives over to Him by obeying His Word fully, we start experiencing the fullness of what God has planned for us. When our focus becomes who we are in Christ, and we have a longing in our hearts through our new nature for what God desires, then we come to the realization that life is designed around God and His Glory and not ourselves. Our existence should be underpinned with this understanding.

God takes care of all of our needs as we learn to trust Him. This is absolutely incredible! How does this compare to anything else in all of life? The only catch is that you have to learn to trust Him completely. In other words, exercise your faith, and not fear. As you begin to see and understand that all the problems in life started when Satan deceived Adam and Eve, then we can begin the journey back to God and a Holy state of being.

As a result of the Fall, man incurred the penalty of death both physically and—more importantly—spiritually. In other words, if you are not a born-again Christian, you are spiritually dead! When it comes to knowing God personally, you have no pulse. You are a human being that God has loaned breath to for a short time. I urge you to act today while you still have an opportunity.

Since the Fall of mankind, sin has run its course. It will continue to do so until an appointed time, then God will end it. He will separate His sheep from the goats. When you consider your life today, you are either a part of the problem and contributing to the mess, or you are growing in Christlikeness, and becoming a greater vessel for God and His Glory. There are only two choices, as Matthew 7 states:

> [13] "Enter through the narrow gate; for the gate is wide and the way is broad that leads to destruction, and there are
>
> many who enter through it. [14] For the gate is small and the way is narrow that leads to life, and there are few who find it (Matthew 7:13–14 New American Standard Bible 1995).

In John 3, Jesus tells us we must be born again:

> [3] Jesus answered and said to him, "Truly, truly, I say to you, unless one is born again he cannot see the kingdom of God." (John 3:3 New American Standard Bible 1995).

And here again, Jesus is giving us a very serious

warning:

> [21] "Not everyone who says to Me, 'Lord, Lord,' will enter the kingdom of heaven, but he who does the will of My Father who is in heaven will enter. [22] Many will say to Me on that day, 'Lord, Lord, did we not prophesy in Your name, and in Your name cast out demons, and in Your name perform many miracles?' [23] And then I will declare to them, 'I never knew you; depart from Me, you who practice lawlessness.' (Matthew 7:21–23 New American Standard Bible 1995).

I urge you to meditate on these verses for as long as it takes. Think long and hard about what He said. Especially, "And then I will declare to them, 'I never knew you; depart from me, you who practice lawlessness."

We're talking about a really serious relationship here. Every second of every day. Not some distant one when you only seek God when you are in a pickle.

Every day that we awaken is a gift from God! Job echoes this truth:

> [1] "Man, who is born of woman,
> Is short-lived and full of turmoil (Job

14:1 New American Standard Bible 1995).

It would be incredible to know what goes through people's minds when they are about to literally take their last breath. On November 27, 2022, my wife and I both tested positive for covid. In the first couple days, there were three times when I could barely breathe. I had next to zero air exchange. I sat up all night in bed with my precious wife and a dear sister in Christ by my side as they were praying, singing, and praising the Lord. *Just incredible!* The stuff I was coughing up was as thick as paste. When you can't breathe, you want one thing, and that is to breathe. By the grace of God, after the first week I began to get better. On December 12, 2022, we retested and were negative.

If you are a true born-again Christion, you have personally been justified by God, and need not fear His condemnation. And having been chosen by God, you don't need to fear His rejection either. And with Christ as your Shepherd, you don't need to fear the valley of the shadow of death. And with the Maker of Heaven and earth watching over you, you don't need to fear anything in life whatsoever; no matter what it is. If you're not used to praising God every day, it's time to start!

Life is very precious! When your hourglass

runs out of sand, you can't just flip it over and start again. It doesn't work that way. Imagine your last day on this earth. Right before you breathe your last breath, you look around your bedside and the realization hits you of exactly what kind of son, daughter, husband, wife, parent, grandparent, family member, friend, or neighbor you were in this life.

From there you will think of unfinished business such as asking someone for forgiveness for something you've done. Have you allowed your pride to get the best of you? And then your thoughts might shift to the people who will be standing around your gravesite as family and friends gather together to show respect and quietly reflect on your life. What will they privately think of you?

At this stage, the time has come that God warned us all about. Eternity is without beginning or end. Whatever your life stood for will be accounted to you forever. Either Heaven or hell. Don't let the day go by without asking God for the forgiveness of your sins as you place your faith in Christ's death and Resurrection alone for your Salvation!

This only represents some of the things that will matter to you most. At the point when you are about to leave this planet, you will either be rejoicing peacefully—knowing you have completed the work God had for you—or you will wish you had done things very differently. Meanwhile, all the different reasons that motivate people to do the wrong thing in this life will be a thing of the past. And they will be left with the realization that judgement day has arrived, and there's no way out.

God gave us all a conscience to help us discern our way through life. When we choose to exercise forgiveness, compassion, love, and grace, we open the door to healing and transformation. The sad thing is many people go to their grave holding on to things that could have been resolved beginning with the simple phrase, "Please forgive me, I was wrong."

For many people, when they're alive and able, their focus is mostly on themselves. And when they are about to pass into eternity, their focus often turns to loved ones and, sometimes for the first time in their lives, they begin to take God a lot more seriously. The family members who are left behind once you've passed are now left to deal with lingering questions like, "What if we would have done things differently?" Depending on the situation, false guilt can often accompany them for the rest of their lives. Years ago, I heard of a woman who walked the halls of her nursing home repeating the phase, "It's all my fault, it's all my fault."

My intention in sharing this is not to upset you, but to cause you to start to live your life differently. We just don't take the time to do what we know to do in our hearts, and we rationalize instead. I encourage you today to pick up the phone, write a letter, or jump in your car and reach out to a loved one while you can. You'll be glad you did.

I called my dad recently. I am ashamed to say, I did so in an effort to call his bluff. To my shock and great joy, he took my call, and we had a beautiful exchange. Before we hung up, I asked him if we could come visit him. He said yes, and we scheduled a visit. We hadn't talked for twenty-five years. To hear his voice was just wonderful!

Michelle and I, along with my two sisters, went to visit him and his second wife on their farm. We had a wonderful visit! He shared an experience he had had the previous winter when his water pipes froze up. To keep his animals hydrated, he carried around two hundred gallons of water to the barn. But then he said, "I can't do it anymore," and he dropped to his knees and cried out to God for help. He said the water pipes thawed instantly, and the water began to flow.

I saw tears running down his face a half a dozen times during our visit. We hugged and kissed each other on the cheek. He prayed to receive Christ as his Savior and Lord! We gave him a Bible as a gift. Just incredible! He agreed to get together again. When I asked him if we could talk more about the Lord, he said yes.

Since then, we have visited three more times, and were planning on getting together again soon, until we heard he had to move into a nursing home. He just turned eighty-four years old. His wife is eighty-eight years old.

I remember several years ago we stopped on a couple occasions to say hello, but we were unable to talk to my dad. My wife Michelle had walked out back to see if she could see him. When she saw some of his equipment parked in the field, she went over and laid hands on the equipment and prayed for his safety as well as his salvation. Praise God for His Amazing Grace! Never stop believing.

On one of our most recent visits, he said he'll shut his dozer down to take a little break to pray for a while. He said to us, "I need to change some things."

A few weeks before our breakthrough with my dad, we shared the Gospel with one of my younger brothers and he prayed to receive Christ as his Savior and Lord. Praise God! It's been a great summer, and things are only going to get better! We all have regrets in this life—God knows I've had my share. I've missed the boat many times, on many fronts. Our family is hurting. The question that we need to answer today is: are we in the process of healing broken relationships around us? Make amends with family members and neighbors. Above all, repent and ask the Lord's forgiveness.

CHAPTER NINE: SPIRITUAL WARFARE IS VERY REAL

[10] Finally, be strong in the Lord and in the strength of His might. [11] Put on the full armor of God, so that you will be able to stand firm against the schemes of the devil. [12] For our struggle is not against flesh and blood, but against the rulers, against the powers, against the world forces of this darkness, against the spiritual forces of wickedness in the heavenly places. [13] Therefore, take up the full armor of God, so that you will be able to resist in the evil day, and having done everything, to stand firm. [14] Stand firm therefore, having girded your loins with truth, and having put on the breastplate of righteousness, [15] and having shod your feet with the preparation of the gospel of peace; [16]

in addition to all, taking up the shield of faith with which you will be able to extinguish all the flaming arrows of the evil one. [17] And take the helmet of salvation, and the sword of the Spirit, which is the word of God (Ephesians 6:10–17 New American Standard Bible 1995).

This passage is *immensely important* when it comes to spiritual warfare and experiencing true victory in your life. It starts out by telling us where our strength really comes from (and it's not found in ourselves). It comes directly from God Almighty through the Power of the Holy Spirit who is living in you if you are a true born-again Christian. As you submit to Him in the moment, you will experience the power of God working in your life. From there you simply repeat the process. As you submit and obey, you are being transformed into Christlikeness. Your protection, wisdom, and maturity follow as a result of an abiding life in Christ producing much fruit for God's Glory.

The passage goes on to tell us why this is so important. It implores us to stand firm against the schemes of the devil. Only by putting on the Full Armor of God and (keeping it on) will you experience great triumph in your life. Let's take a look at the spiritual weapons God has given us as

Christians to stand firm against Satan and his evil cohorts who are set on destroying our lives.

The Helmet of Salvation. Your mind is the battlefield where the real war is being waged. Once you have come to faith in Christ, you are able to discern the truth from a lie. The helmet is designed to protect our new way of thinking that is based on God's Holy Word. If your mind becomes susceptible to one of Satan's lies, your life is greatly affected. And if your mind is neutralized, you are rendered mostly ineffective. That means we have to be on guard. We cannot allow Satan's lies to lodge in our thoughts and cause us to respond to things in an un-Christlike way. This is about our daily protection and deliverance from the devil's consistent attacks. He tries to cause us to doubt our Salvation through discouragement and fear. Satan wants to rob us of our hope in Christ. He wants us to drop the ball on our relationship with God and turn back to our old ways. Take every thought captive to the obedience of Christ. Stand firm. The only influence Satan has in our lives is what we allow!

The Breastplate of Righteousness. As Christians, righteousness is our foremost protection against Satan and his deceptive schemes. By living a righteous life, we minimize the numerous ways he can attack us. When honesty and purity are a way of life, and you long to follow Christ's example, you are positioning yourself for greater and greater victory. So, your daily righteousness becomes your spiritual breastplate that helps you guard against the enemy's attacks. During these times, a righteous response protects us from his designed lies to destroy our lives. See examples of this in God's Word in the following verses:

> [7] Submit therefore to God. Resist the devil and he will flee from you (James 4:7 New American Standard Bible 1995).

> [27] Be angry, and yet do not sin; do not let the sun go down on your anger, and do not give the devil an opportunity (Ephesians 4:26–27 New American Standard Bible 1995).

The passage above is referring to righteous anger, which is being angry at what makes God angry. God's anger is a result of His righteousness against all sin and evil in the world.

The Belt of Truth. Truth is what sets us free from all of the lies meant to deceive, divide, and destroy us. Whether you are confronting Satan's attempts to cause you to distrust God, or your flesh is rising up, remember that truth is on your side. You have the ability and opportunity to make the right decisions. A lying tongue is detestable to God, but when truth is applied, peace is the result, and victory is ours. This triumph is, of course, the beginning of Christlikeness. Applying and adhering to God's Word is the key to everything. Our job is to immediately apply it. If you are a follower of Jesus Christ, your confidence comes from your relationship with Him. He has secured your victory. Stand firm therefore!

> [5] I am the vine, you are the branches; he who abides in Me and I in him, he bears much fruit, for apart from Me you can do nothing (John 15:5 New American Standard Bible 1995).

The Shoes of Peace. Satan has put many obstacles in the path of Christian believers who are growing in their faith. He is afraid of what you are becoming. He wants to prevent you from fulfilling your ministry. Worry is opposed by peace. Satan uses fear and anxiety to try to get us triggered and off track. If we fail to recognize it for what it is, then we lose our peace, strongholds kick in, and we get stuck. It is a conditioned reaction hardwired into us as children until we realize what is actually happening and why, and correct the way we choose to respond. Nobody can say, "My circumstances plus anxiety, fear, and anger will improve my life."

Where do you stand today? Are you seeking freedom from your past, or are you happy with the way things are going? Search your heart. Do you have true peace in your life? Oneness with the Lord through a personal relationship based on Biblical truth is what brings peace to your soul. The Gospel of peace keeps our feet grounded. You can begin to experience it today by placing your faith in Christ alone. From there you will be fully armed and able to stand firm and hold your ground while being at complete peace. There is a reason peace is included as one of the fruits of the Spirit. Get excited as you read the following verse:

> [27] Peace, I leave with you; My peace I give to you; not as the world gives do I give to you. Do not let your heart be troubled, nor let it be fearful (John 14:27 New American Standard Bible 1995).

The Sword of the Spirit. God has armed us as believers with the only weapon we need. That is the Word of God, and it is more powerful than anything else in life! When applied correctly, it fends off Satan's attacks and allows us to rejoice in our Lord. In other words, pull your sword out and use it immediately. When you are being tempted by the enemy, do you stand your ground based on God's Word, or do you allow him to stomp on your feet? If you have backslidden in your walk with

God, ask Him for His forgiveness, and get back on track. Go on offense today. You won't regret it! Always remember Jesus' example to us in the wilderness:

> [1] Then Jesus was led up by the Spirit into the wilderness to be tempted by the devil. [2] And after He had fasted forty days and forty nights, He then became hungry. [3] And the tempter came and said to Him, "If You are the Son of God, command that these stones become bread." [4] But He answered and said, "It is written, 'Man shall not live on bread alone, but on every word that proceeds out of the mouth of God.'"
>
> [5] Then the devil took Him into the holy city and had Him stand on the pinnacle of the temple, [6] and said to Him, "If You are the Son of God, throw Yourself down; for it is written,
> 'He will command His angels concerning You';
> and
> 'On their hands they will bear You up,
> So that You will not strike Your foot against a stone.'"
>
> [7] Jesus said to him, "On the other hand,

it is written, 'You shall not put the Lord your God to the test.'"

[8] Again, the devil took Him to a very high mountain and showed Him all the kingdoms of the world and their glory; [9] and he said to Him, "All these things I will give You, if You fall down and worship me." [10] Then Jesus said to him, "Go, Satan! For it is written, 'You shall worship the Lord your God, and serve Him only.'" [11] Then the devil left Him; and behold, angels came and began to minister to Him (Matthew 4:1–11 New American Standard Bible 1995).

The Shield of Faith. Our personal trust in God Almighty is our shield of protection. When Satan's flaming arrows are coming at you, you can stand firm based on God's written promises found in His Word. There are a lot of things in life you can't fully trust, but God is not one of them. If God wasn't real, we would have no hope at all, but thankfully that's not the case. When we place our faith in Him, our needs are covered. He will deflect Satan's fiery arrows, which are intended to harm us. We just have to exercise our faith and believe. If you are struggling in your faith today, you are listening to the wrong voice in your head. You must filter everything through the Word of God. He did not complicate this for us. We ourselves complicate it when we fail to believe. Remember, the truth sets us free:

> [1] Now faith is the assurance of things hoped for, the conviction of things not seen (Hebrews 11:1 New American Standard Bible 1995).

> [27] My sheep hear My voice, and I know them, and they follow Me; [28] and I give eternal life to them, and they will never perish; and no one will snatch them out of My hand (John 10:27–28 New American Standard Bible 1995).

Satan seeks to destroy a believer's assurance of Salvation, which is not possible because it is eternally protected by God's promises. That doesn't mean Satan will give up. That means we can expect to be attacked by his lies and deceptions for the rest of our lives here on earth. In order to effectively counter Satan's relentless schemes, Christians need to understand how to win the battle. We do that by allowing God full access to every area of our thoughts. God's Word speaks truth into our hearts and minds, which changes our perspective on life, and frees us from all forms of sin. Take lust for example, or any other form of temptation. You have to cut it off immediately. Stop entertaining it. See it for what it is: ungodly garbage holding you back from being transformed into Christlikeness, enabling you to fulfill your ministry for God's Glory! When Jesus walked this earth, He was fully God and fully man. Just because He is not with us physically any longer, it doesn't mean He is not present. God lives in the spiritual realm. Satan exists in the spiritual realm. Both are very real. It's time we get real about this before it's too late.

> [1] He who dwells in the shelter of the Most High Will abide in the shadow of the Almighty (Psalm 91:1 New American Standard Bible 1995).

Satan is an angelic being who, because of his beauty and status, became full of pride and rebelled against God. Because of that, he fell from his position in Heaven, and is now the ruler of this world. The following verses describe his fall.

> [13] "But you said in your heart,
> 'I will ascend to heaven;
> I will raise my throne above the stars of God,
> And I will sit on the mount of assembly
> In the recesses of the north.
> [14] 'I will ascend above the heights of the clouds;

I will make myself like the Most High.' (Isaiah 14:13–14 New American Standard Bible 1995).

Since his fall, Satan has been relentless in his attempts to subvert God's will. Although he knows it is completely impossible, he still tries his best. He counterfeits everything that God does to gain the worship of this fallen world and to encourage greater opposition to God's Kingdom. What side are you currently on? Your answer to this question has eternal ramifications!

Just like Adam and Eve were deceived by Satan, we too have all been deceived countless times by the enemy. One third of the angels sided with Satan, and God kicked them all out of Heaven. Since then, they have been doing everything possible to cause havoc in our lives. Just like God gave you and I a free will, all the angels in Heaven have a free will. Don't buy the lie. The devil is not at all like he is portrayed half of the time. He is not this innocent little guy sitting on your shoulder whispering nice things into your ear. He wants to take you and as many other people as possible to hell with him.

The name Satan means "adversary". He wars against everyone united with God. That means if you are a Christian, you have a target on your back. The name devil means "accuser". Therefore, we need to be very intentional to discern the different voices that pop into our heads every day. If Satan can control how you think, he will naturally control your life, undermining your walk with God. We take charge of this by taking every thought captive to the obedience of Christ. The thoughts that pop into your head are either consistent with the Bible or they are not. If they are, praise God and press on in faith. If not, you simply cast it out of your mind in Jesus' Mighty Name, Amen. You have to love God's Word. It truly does set you free.

> [3] For though we walk in the flesh, we do not war according to the flesh, [4] for the weapons of our warfare are not of the flesh, but divinely powerful for the destruction of fortresses. [5] We are destroying speculations and every lofty thing raised up against the knowledge of God, and we are taking every thought captive to the obedience of Christ (2 Corinthians 10:3–5 New American Standard Bible 1995).

Another word for "fortress" mentioned above is stronghold. This is another terrible result of the fall of mankind. Satan sets up different strongholds in our minds while we are growing up as kids. In doing so, he aims to control the way we perceive things—what we believe or don't believe. Our perspective on life. How we view right from wrong. How we think and act. Our attitudes. The way we treat others. Needless to say, strongholds are powerful. That's why the passage above says, "For the weapons of our warfare are not of the flesh, but divinely powerful for the destruction of fortresses." God is telling us to destroy all strongholds in our minds by replacing them with God's Word alone. Has that been your focus? If it hasn't been, you need to reprioritize. Why would God say that if it wasn't necessary? He is trying to set us free from Satan's schemes that, if left unchecked, will destroy our lives.

Have you ever had a terrible thought enter into your head out of nowhere? I can answer that for you, and I don't even know you. The answer is yes, you have, because that's the way it works. Adam and Eve didn't have those kinds of thoughts before the Fall. Born-again Christians will not have these kinds of thoughts in Heaven. This is a real battle for the here and now. You can't expect to experience great victories in this life if you are not very intentional concerning spiritual warfare. Just ignoring it will not make it go away.

The problem is that we as human beings get so caught up with all the things here on earth that we give little to no attention to what's actually going on in the spiritual realm, and how it directly affects our lives every day! In doing so, we are missing a critical part of the puzzle, which explains why we stay stuck on first base, both in our walk with God and every other relationship. You simply cannot function at a higher level without learning to discern Satan's deceptions and proactively anticipate his attacks. You must learn to immediately discern the devil's lies and deceptions in the moment in order to overcome all the effects that they have on our lives. This couldn't be any more serious! Think about how this affects your marriage, your children, and everything else that is dear to you.

Prior to covid, my wife Michelle and I experienced eight straight years of weekly date days. We had a wonderful time and grew a lot in our marriage together. But there was still something that was holding us back from further growth. It was at that time when God answered my prayers, and clearly put two specific things on my heart. One was agape love, which is how God loves us, and the second was spiritual warfare.

I have heard of both of these topics mentioned on and off over the years, but I never dug deep like I should have. I never recognized the huge importance of applying it to our marriage every day, all day! Today, I fully believe these two subjects need to be emphasized as absolute necessities, along with the verse below:

^{24} For this reason a man shall leave his father and his mother, and be joined to his wife; and they shall become one flesh (Genesis 2:24 New American Standard Bible 1995).

If you are attending premarital, marriage, family, or individual counseling, request that these topics be discussed in depth. Remember, there is wisdom in a multitude of counsel. This was life changing for my wife and I, and I promise it will be for you too. Do your homework.

Because the battle is being waged in our minds, we need to take every thought captive to the obedience of Christ. To do this, we need to first slow down and be at peace by placing all our faith and trust in God. When we allow people or our circumstances to control our reactions to something, we are handing over control of our lives. What precedes a person's emotions? Feelings. What precedes a person's feelings? Thoughts. What precedes a person's thoughts? Nothing. That is why God said to take every thought captive concerning strongholds. This action enables you to discern the truth and make a wise decision in the moment. This enables you to apply God's truth to your situation, which then results in the destruction of the strongholds controlling your life. If this process is repeated continually, then great healing and transformation into Christlikeness will come upon your life. That should be very exciting for you! The key is to live in God's Word!

No matter what you are going through, no matter what your future holds, God loves and cares about us all perfectly. My precious wife Michelle and I have been around and around the mountain. We could have simply given up a thousand times, but we haven't, and we never will. We have personally and intimately experienced God's Word in action. We fully submitted and obeyed Him when it really mattered, and you can't forget an experience like that. Admittedly, we do not do it perfectly every single time. But we are experiencing a clear pattern of continual healing and growth like never before. Praise God Almighty!

> [3] "The steadfast of mind You will keep in perfect peace,
> Because he trusts in You.
>
> [4] "Trust in the Lord forever,
> For in God the Lord, we have an everlasting Rock (Isaiah 26:3–4 New American Standard Bible 1995).
>
> [17] And the work of righteousness will be peace,
> And the service of righteousness,

quietness and confidence forever (Isaiah 32:17 New American Standard Bible 1995).

We all have to be very intentional about this! This is a full-time job with countless benefits. If you are not already, think of what you could be modeling to your precious spouse and children that will bless them greatly. Instead of continuing to get frustrated with each other, immediately come to each other's defense, exactly what our Lord would have us do! The key is to truly meditate on God's Word daily. To this end, it is best if you memorize Scripture, then simply apply it in faith and trust God for the results.

> [1] How blessed is the man who does not walk in the counsel of the wicked,
> Nor stand in the path of sinners,
> Nor sit in the seat of scoffers!
>
> [2] But his delight is in the law of the Lord,
> And in His law he meditates day and night.
>
> [3] He will be like a tree firmly planted by streams of water,
> Which yields its fruit in its season
> And its leaf does not wither;
> And in whatever he does, he prospers (Psalm 1:1–3 New American Standard Bible 1995).

Take time to break every verse down word-by-word and apply it exactly the way God intended for us to do so. This has to become the norm every day! Just like you would prepare for a test.

> [15] A gentle answer turns away wrath,
> But a harsh word stirs up anger (Proverbs 15:1 New American Standard Bible 1995).

We have to be wise about this! You can't defeat an enemy that you're not willing to confront. It is important to memorize Scripture because you can't just say, "Pardon me Satan, I need to find my Bible, along with the rest of my armor."

Depending on your approach, it will amaze you how you can have total and complete peace throughout the whole process. It gives you real hope and excitement. Especially knowing you are truly growing in your faith, and that it is pleasing to God. Glory be to His name!

Don't just double down, triple down—say to yourself, no matter what it is, it's not worth grieving the Holy Spirit! If we can't manage life at an average level of difficulty (spiritually speaking) how will we ever manage life when all hell breaks loose? Learn to see all this other stuff as preparation for the main event that is coming very soon!

Remember, you can't fence time. Another year will go by before you know it. I have the letters "WWJD" (What Would Jesus Do) taped to the hutch of my desk. It is intentionally positioned directly in front of me all day long. So, each time you face a new situation, ask yourself, "What would Jesus do"? Well, we know He prayed to God the Father at all times. That means He would express unconditional love, joy, peace, patience, kindness, goodness, faithfulness, gentleness, and self-control. He would also forgive when asked. He would reach out to help no matter what the need. That's why we as Christians are to model Christ's love more and more each day.

> [17] The merciful man does himself good,
> But the cruel man does himself harm (Proverbs 11:17 New American Standard Bible 1995).

One very important thing to keep in mind through this process is that Satan designed strongholds either to try to keep you from knowing God, or to try to undermine your relationship with Him. He does this by trying to cause you to sin and stay stuck all while he is accusing you of being a terrible person not worthy of God's love. When I was first going through this, it rattled me. I felt off track for a few years until I learned more about all of this, and actually worked through the process of what was really going on. Now I can quickly recognize it for what it is and see through it. This is all part of a Christian's journey to greater understanding, freedom, and peace. But before we can experience that, we have to overcome all the thoughts, feelings, and emotions that we can't help but feel initially. Things like grief, shame, and embarrassment that you feel because of the thoughts that pop into your head before a Holy and Righteous God. What really helped me was going back to the truth found in God's Word. Remember, the truth sets you free. The Bible tells us that Jesus was fully God and fully man.

> [5] Have this attitude in yourselves which was also in Christ Jesus, [6] who, although He existed in the form of God, did not regard equality with God a thing to be grasped, [7] but emptied Himself, taking the form of a bond-servant, and being made in the likeness of men (Philippians 2:5–7 New American Standard Bible 1995).

Jesus also experienced Satan's thought bullets, but He never allowed it to divert Him from doing the Father's will. The point is, God knows the kinds of attacks we are under, and that Satan is behind it all. We simply have to accept that God understands and that He will provide a way of escape.

> [13] No temptation has overtaken you but such as is common to man; and God is faithful, who will not allow you to be tempted beyond what you are able, but with the temptation will provide the way of escape also, so that you will be able to endure it (1 Corinthians 10:13 New American Standard Bible 1995).

Another element of this battle is that Satan is very jealous of God. The Bible tells us pride comes before our fall, and that is exactly what happened to Satan. As I mentioned before, he became full of pride and wanted to become like God. When that didn't happen, he set out to rob God of His Glory. We as Christians who truly love the Lord cannot continue to allow that to happen when it is in our power to stop it. All we have to do is trust God by submitting to His written Word. We cannot continue to be deceived by Satan. He is our worst enemy. It is time we wake up and get our hearts and minds fixed on God and things above. Spiritual warfare is a battle between good and evil. Between God and His children, which is the true Church, and Satan and his children.

¹⁰ By this the children of God and the children of the devil are obvious: anyone who does not practice righteousness is not of God, nor the one who does not love his brother (1 John 3:10 New American Standard Bible 1995).

If fulfilling your ministry for God's Glory is your main goal as a Christian, which it should be, then understanding spiritual warfare must be a focal point. We have to ask ourselves if we're better off going through life with both eyes fully open or half closed. Satan wants us to remain ignorant about the truth because the truth sets us free. The truth is our friend that leads us to great revelation. It gives us wisdom and insight into the world around us. It teaches us great lessons about life. It blesses our relationships because they are healthier and are able to grow much deeper as a result. If you are not experiencing freedom, then you are perhaps not applying truth properly. Truth has no agenda. Maybe you feel like you've exhausted your patience—but have you exhausted study and prayer?

If experiencing true love, joy, and peace is a longing of yours, then you will have to learn how to love first. And this is not possible without learning all about spiritual warfare because a natural consequence of spiritual warfare is deception, division, and destruction. That is why people stay stuck in unhealthy relationships for decades. They lack the necessary tools to repair their marriages and other relationships. Then it gets passed on to the next generation. Then they themselves continue to try to stick a square peg in a round hole for however long, which is all avoidable if we are determined to put a stop to it.

There's an old saying that says, "Experience is the hardest teacher. It gives the test first and then the lesson." The tests are all the trials in life. The lesson is we can't do it alone. Humility tells us we are dependent on God. Pride tells us we can do it alone. Realize your dependence on God and you will become stronger with every trial you tackle on your knees.

Years ago, my wife Michelle and I discovered that most of the time we got into an argument, it was due to a misunderstanding. When we would circle back around and discuss the details of the argument, it tracked back to a simple misunderstanding. That is the prince of the power of the air. It is the devil's plan to build up walled fortifications around people's hearts and minds, and he starts to do so very early on in our lives. Again, that is where taking every thought captive to the obedience of Christ is huge! When something doesn't seem right, simply clarify it to avoid Satan's lies.

Take some time and list the top ten most important lessons you've learned in your life. Think about everything up to this moment in time. What would you change if you could do it all over again? Have you sought counseling? Counseling is not for dummies, like some people think. The Bible tells us there is wisdom in a multitude of counsel. Think about the things you know you have done wrong but continued because you were not sure how to fix it. That's the benefit of wise counsel. Once applied, our lives are simplified. We can walk in greater wisdom and insight. That improves all our relationships and simplifies our lives so we can focus on fulfilling our ministries.

> [22] Without consultation, plans are frustrated,
> But with many counselors they succeed (Proverbs 15:22 New American Standard Bible 1995).
>
> [20] Listen to counsel and accept discipline,
> That you may be wise the rest of your days (Proverbs 19:20 New American Standard Bible 1995).

God has given us all the answers to meet our every need, care, and concern. All we have to do is pick up a Bible and read it. Then pray in faith, trusting and believing in the One True God. If we do that, He will reward our faith and walk alongside us every single step of the way. This is His desire. He loves us in a Holy and Perfect way. Who doesn't want that? Don't take my word for it, see what He Himself says in the verse below:

> [7] If you abide in Me, and My words abide in you, ask whatever you wish, and it will be done for you (John 15:7 New American Standard Bible 1995).

We have to be willing to exchange our will for God's will. Another way it is commonly stated is that we have to die to self. We have to lay our lives down, pick up our cross, and follow Christ. It is no longer I who live, but Christ who lives in me. Is that your mindset every day? As you learn to trust Him in all things, you bring glory and honor to His name. You also become conformed to His likeness. Then, as you continue to grow in your faith and understanding, you share that with others, beginning with your family, friends, neighbors, and others. It's very exciting. I know for myself and my wife, we absolutely love to share with others because we are excited for them to experience God's Grace, Mercies, Wisdom, and Power. When you go through life and don't have the answers to problems you are experiencing, it leaves you with little hope. But when you have experienced it firsthand, you know that if people intentionally apply the truth, great changes await them. Nothing compares to God's Holy design.

Secondly, He says, "[If] My words abide in you." This is where you must replace all your usual responses to life circumstances with God's Word. Over your lifetime, however old you may be, you have accumulated for yourself certain thought patterns and reactions to address various issues. The problem is that if your response isn't Christlike, then you are not applying God's Word correctly. The result is that you will stay stuck where you are, and if you are married and have children, all they are seeing and experiencing is the same old thing. When you look in the mirror every morning, intentionally pause and ask yourself, what has really changed in my life that would be considered significant? It has to be directly linked to God and the teaching of the Bible as it relates to your personal healing, transformation, and fulfilling your ministry. God has a plan for your life. Are you on track with that plan, or are you missing the boat? Trust me, it is all that is going to matter in the end!

CHAPTER TEN: WHAT IS YOUR GO-TO?

One of Satan's main objectives is to keep us stuck in dysfunctional lifestyles and relationships. If you are a Christian, make no mistake, the devil is trying everything possible to undermine your personal relationship with God. The devil's plan is to prevent the Lord's will from manifesting in your life.

The enemy knows our weaknesses. He intentionally tries to keep us off track in an effort to keep us from growing in Christlikeness. He doesn't want us to fulfill our ministry as Christians. The catch is, if we continue to be deceived, then we cannot grow in Christlikeness. That means we obviously cannot fulfill our ministries for God's Glory! In turn, we then cannot effectively become the salt and the light for God's Glory in this ever-darkening world that desperately needs to hear the truth in order to be set free.

> [13] "You are the salt of the earth; but if the salt has become tasteless, how can it

be made salty again? It is no longer good for anything, except to be thrown out and trampled underfoot by men.

[14] "You are the light of the world. A city set on a hill cannot be hidden; [15] nor does anyone light a lamp and put it under a basket, but on the lampstand, and it gives light to all who are in the house. [16] Let your light shine before men in such a way that they may see your good works, and glorify your Father who is in heaven (Matthew 5:13–16 New American Standard Bible 1995).

Another thing Satan is working hard at is to keep us from passing our faith on to the next generation, and he has been very successful. He would rather we wear our Christianity on our sleeves. Going to church is ok, just so you only want your ears tickled, or you're listening to false teachers or following false religions.

Think back over the past year. What do you do to manage your thoughts and emotions that can quickly lead to fear if not delt with correctly? Do you pray through it in faith? Do you meditate on certain verses to be at peace? Or do you turn your TV on and grab some comfort food and a glass of alcohol to try to forget about life for a while? What is your *conditioned* reaction? How would your spouse, child, or best friend answer this question for you?

If you drink alcohol, have you fully considered your reasoning behind it? Not just a quick answer that supports your personal desires, but the real truth based on facts. People claim they drink for different reasons, but the biggest motive is to numb themselves from various hurts, fears, and frustrations from Satan's previous lies and deceptions.

At the root of this, we try to keep our pain out of our awareness from one day to the next. This explains how alcoholism becomes a lifestyle and why it is one of Satan's favorite weapons— not to mention illegal drugs. If it was so helpful, doctors would be prescribing it left and right. Our families and society would be very healthy as a result. This is obviously not the case. Like the old saying goes, "The devil is in the bottle."

> [6] "Forsake your folly and live,
> And proceed in the way of understanding." (Proverbs 9:6 New American Standard Bible 1995).

So, whether it was different things you went through growing up, or as an adult, they are indicators that something much deeper is going on that needs to be addressed in a very sincere and logical way. The wisest way to do that is to address the root of the problem, not just the symptoms.

Another reason people drink is to give them a false sense of confidence over their personal fears and insecurities, which is the same as pretending. You may also be seeking to fit in with others. To be accepted. Alcohol becomes a convenient distraction from life's many challenges and difficulties, and if the cycle isn't broken, then it continues from bad to worse. Usually passing it on to your children and grandchildren and everybody loses. This is not a legacy you want to leave behind.

It's pretty rare that a person just has one glass of wine or beer. It's like coffee. You don't stop until you're feeling the caffein. Or should I say, not feeling it if you are continuing to run away from your unresolved problems. Back to pretending. And why does it continue? Because you have neglected the application of God's Word in all areas of your life.

Have you ever thought deep down inside that you may be attempting to medicate yourself as a way to cope with different fears in your life? Instead of trusting the Lord, this is the best thing you have been able to come up with. It's a way of hiding really. It's an irrational way of avoiding the worthy cost of being all in for Christ. I believe this is far more prevalent than people are willing to admit. Even for those of us who acknowledge ourselves as followers of Jesus Christ and attend church every week. It's similar in some ways to the percentage of the population around the world who used food regularly to comfort themselves before it was ever known as comfort food.

I grew up in a family of alcoholics. My dad was an alcoholic for many years. Growing up, most of my friends drank a lot. I had two older friends that died of cirrhosis of the liver. My grandparents on my mom's side owned a bar before my time. And my aunt and uncle owned a bar right down the street from them a generation later—an establishment I basically grew up in. As I mentioned before, I had my first beer at age nine. I too became an alcoholic until I was in my mid-twenties when I was injured. *Unrelated.*

There have been three different times over the years when I went through a season of drinking. The first time was before I remarried. I was living in my apartment as a baby Christian. I would drink a few beers here and there. It was short lived. I was having company one day, and I was embarrassed that it was sitting in my refrigerator. I asked my caregiver to push it toward the back to hide it from their view. She responded, "Don't be a hypocrite, either drink or don't drink." I was grateful for her forthrightness. I had her dump it down the drain. At the same time, I gave Jean, an older caregiver (in her fifties) a half a dozen playboy magazines to take home to burn in her burning barrel. This is yet another example of Satan's evil schemes. That's how something so precious that God created for us to enjoy as married couples, has been used to pervert our society to no end. All this type of stuff keeps us from God's best! Pray and ask God for His forgiveness no matter what it is! Then pray for wisdom on how best to move forward.

> [3] Be gracious to me, O Lord,
> For to You I cry all day long.
>
> [4] Make glad the soul of Your servant,
> For to You, O Lord, I lift up my soul.
>
> [5] For You, Lord, are good, and ready to forgive,
> And abundant in lovingkindness to all who call upon You.
>
> [6] Give ear, O LORD, to my prayer;
> And give heed to the voice of my supplications!
>
> [7] In the day of my trouble I shall call upon You,
> For You will answer me (Psalm 86:3–7 New American Standard Bible 1995).

The second season of drinking occurred many years later when I felt our marriage was not progressing like we needed, and we didn't have the answers. At that time, I would have a couple glasses of wine twice a week for about a year.

The third time I returned to alcohol happened a decade after that. We were still stuck without a gameplan to heal and grow in our faith and marriage in a real significant way. Squabbling every week got old. At the time, we were going out to eat more often and I would have two or three glasses of wine. On one occasion, I had seven glasses of wine and threw up. The incident reminded me of when I was a kid. After drinking, half the time I found myself hugging the toilet. What a sad way to live life as a child, let alone as an adult. Whether you're throwing up somewhere or staying stuck on first base for the rest of your life, what's the difference?

Anybody who has ever drank alcohol knows it doesn't change anything. It only makes things worse, and in spite of that, we continue to do it anyway. That's right where Satan wants us. I stopped drinking again on September 18, 2018, and I have had no desire to go back to it. We are at a place in our marriage that we have never been before, and we are only going to keep growing and maturing because of the new revelations God continues to show us. We must be determined to stay the course. God's grace is sufficient for us. Praise His Holy and Precious name!

10 "He who is faithful in a very little

thing is faithful also in much; and he who is unrighteous in a very little thing is unrighteous also in much. [11] Therefore if you have not been faithful in the use of unrighteous wealth, who will entrust the true riches to you? [12] And if you have not been faithful in the use of that which is another's, who will give you that which is your own? [13] No servant can serve two masters; for either he will hate the one and love the other, or else he will be devoted to one and despise the other. You cannot serve God and wealth." (Luke 16:10–13 New American Standard Bible 1995).

Our old pastor said once, "Where we go when we're in trouble is what we really believe in." If you still believe alcohol is helpful in any way, it's time to reassess your logic. Remember what I said earlier. If you grew up in a dysfunctional home, you likely learned not to seek comfort through relationships, so we seek it in other ways. Southern Comfort, anyone? This explains in part how we get off track in our relationships. We struggle to reconnect because we never fully learned how to do it the right way to begin with. So, it's not a natural experience we necessarily have, but something we really need to learn in order to improve our lives, as well as train it into our children so they can avoid what we may be going through now. They will then be equipped to pass it on to the grandchildren, turning the whole family in a new direction.

We all must learn how fear works to defeat us in life, and who is behind it. Then we can develop a sound biblical response to it touched on in the previous chapter. There are two distinct dynamics at play here. One is the depth of hurt and pain in each person's heart from their past. The other is the amount of growth and maturity they have experienced as an adult. So, I ask you, if you never had access to alcohol or drugs again, what would you do to replace them that would help you cope with life? A consistent daily accountability partner is huge. Stop going to certain places that encourage unhealthy lifestyles. Stop hanging around people who have no interest in changing their lives for the better. Hang out with Jesus Christ our Savior instead. Raise your arms above your head and give Him praise and thanks for all He has done for us! Then drop your arms down around your shoulders and give Him a big hug showing your love and appreciation for everything He has done for us! Then encourage others to do the same a dozen times a day. Praise His name!

Everyone wants what they don't have because it's easier to imagine than it is to go out and get it for themselves. People prefer quick fixes such as alcohol because it doesn't take any time or effort on their part. Just pop the cork and drift off like everything will be ok. But that's the problem. It's not going to be ok until you change nearly everything about your life. Does anybody really think that being redeemed back into God's Kingdom was not going to cost us everything in this life? That is to be sanctified back into a Holy state of being in Christlikeness. God could not have been any more serious about this! For His part, He went to the Cross to die for our sins to make it possible. Our part is to follow His example. We don't achieve that by continuing in our old ways. We have to keep raising the bar as it pertains to righteousness— instead of continuing to go to the local bar to numb ourselves. Then we have to keep raising the bar, spiritually speaking. None of us went to kindergarten and stayed there. We worked our way up the ladder. As Christians, we do that as we grow in Christlikeness from glory-to-glory-to-glory. Work your way backwards. At the end of your life, what will you wish you would have done differently? Now is your only opportunity. Don't throw away another day.

> [8] My Father is glorified by this, that you bear much fruit, and so prove to be My disciples (John 15:8 New American

Standard Bible 1995).

When you were a kid, maybe you stayed in your bedroom at times to avoid uncomfortable situations. Today it's your workplace, your garage, the golf course, or the corner bar. Anything to avoid what seemed to be the inevitable. Another disagreement with your spouse, child, or someone else that doesn't end well half the time. You didn't want to deal with it because it seemed like there was rarely a win-win solution to the problem. This isn't uncommon, actually. In fact, it's the norm for most families. But it doesn't have to stay this way if you apply God's Word and exercise your faith. Every day you build on the day before. In time, as you stick with it, transformation occurs. Like anything else in life, what you put into it, you will get out of it. After exercising for six months, it's pretty obvious what kind of effort you've put into it. When you receive your grades at the end of the semester, it becomes clear how you spent your time. When your child leaves your home to step out into life, you will ponder what all you did right, and what you should have done differently. Ephesians 4 illustrates the importance of our individual responsibilities:

> [29] Let no unwholesome word proceed from your mouth, but only such a word

as is good for edification according to the need of the moment, so that it will give grace to those who hear. [30] Do not grieve the Holy Spirit of God, by whom you were sealed for the day of redemption. [31] Let all bitterness and wrath and anger and clamor and slander be put away from you, along with all malice. [32] Be kind to one another, tender-hearted, forgiving each other, just as God in Christ also has forgiven you (Ephesians 4:29–32 New American Standard Bible 1995).

Feelings of rejection and abandonment are the two deepest soul wounds we can experience. No matter how much you try to drown the hurt and pain away, it won't work. It doesn't just go away. *It has to be replaced.* The Bible tells us to transform our hearts and renew our minds based on God's Word, through the power of the Holy Spirit. Not with a bottle of booze or some other substance or distraction. Why? Because no one has ever succeeded in doing so. Imagine how much precious time has been completely wasted over a person's lifetime that can never be retrieved. We all have limited opportunities in this life. We must take advantage of every day. Get wise to how Satan operates. Be very careful of the different voices that pop into your head every day. To succeed, you—like everyone else—desperately need God's help to overcome this!

We have all gone through different experiences growing up. Good, bad, or ugly. Maybe you grew up in a better home than your spouse did, or vice versa. How much did you honestly understand about all the in-depth elements of relationships prior to getting married? What have you learned in the meantime? How well did you really know yourself even? Did you have a game plan that extended past your honeymoon? Thorough premarital counseling based on God's Word is very important! If you have children, what have you been modeling into them thus far? Maybe there are some things you would do differently. Much of this doesn't even come out until the first or second year of marriage.

When we choose to continue to respond the same old way that has kept us stuck in a cycle of dysfunction, should we be surprised by the outcome? It's when unhealed or neglected wounds rise up and feel like fresh injuries all over again, and just about everything inside of you wants to respond in a certain way. Deep, open, and honest reflection brings great self-awareness. In time, you will experience a growing realization of what you need to do to heal and grow individually and as a couple. Of course, God will help you navigate difficult decisions if you ask:

> [5] Trust in the LORD with all your heart
> And do not lean on your own understanding.
>
> [6] In all your ways acknowledge Him,
> And He will make your paths straight (Proverbs 3:5–6 New American Standard Bible 1995).

> [7] "Ask, and it will be given to you; seek, and you will find; knock, and it will be opened to you. [8] For everyone who asks receives, and he who seeks finds, and to him who knocks it will be opened (Matthew 7:7–8 New American Standard Bible 1995).

What do you normally do as a couple when one or both of you start to get triggered? This obviously applies to single people as well. Do you have a sound Biblical strategy to counter Satan's attacks, or do you just stand there and argue as you go around the same old mountain? Remember, as adults you are no longer a victim of your past. Depending on how serious we are about making necessary changes as couples, a decade or two or more of our lives can be unwisely wasted. This occurs due to our ignorance, pride, fear, unforgiveness, and lack of discipline. It's completely up to each of us to decide how we will live our lives. We were all created with a free will. The ball is in your court. What is your game plan for the year ahead? Be very specific and intentional. Plan your work, and then work your plan.

> [1] What is the source of quarrels and conflicts among you? Is not the source your pleasures that wage war in your members? [2] You lust and do not have; so you commit murder. You are envious and cannot obtain; so you fight and quarrel. You do not have because you do not ask. [3] You ask and do not receive, because you ask with wrong motives, so that you may spend it on your pleasures (James 4:1–3 New American Standard Bible 1995).

If every married couple suddenly became business partners, we would all find ways to work well together. We would improve our product to better meet needs. We would improve our customer service to build healthy relationships. We would go out of our way every day to run a top-shelf business. And if one of our customers was being a little cranky, we would model Christ's love to them. Hoping and praying that they would come to the truth and be at peace. We all need to learn to go the extra mile—whether it be in our marriages, raising precious children, or loving our neighbor. Unconditional love is what we are all missing and long for in this life. It's time to get off the bench and on to the field. It's time to score some points for our families. It's time to lead and not follow. It's time for change, starting right now!

Was Jesus consumed with doing the Father's will? Yes, He was, and that should be our number one purpose as well!

Jesus came to bring life out of death. Ask yourself, do I really want to continue to take baby steps for the rest of my life? Or do I want to take a step of faith today and fulfill the ministry God has personally designed for me? If history is wrong about this, then you have nothing to lose. But if history is correct, and God is real, then you have *everything* to lose. The forgiveness of your sins, eternal life in Heaven, as well as a glorified body to worship, praise, and serve a Holy God forever— just to mention a few. The Bible says:

> [9] That if you confess with your mouth Jesus as Lord, and believe in your heart that God raised Him from the dead, you will be saved;
>
> [10] for with the heart a person believes,

resulting in righteousness,
and with the mouth he confesses,
resulting in salvation (Romans 10:9–10
New American Standard Bible 1995).

Is your private life different from your public life? Our maturity level from one degree to the next is based on our likeness to Christ and our reactions to everyday circumstances. It's one thing to sound like Christ. It's a whole other thing to model Christ as He would have us. The key to our healing and maturity is to eliminate anything and everything that attempts to replace our faith in Christ alone, and His will and purpose for our lives. This immediately brings us back to spiritual warfare. If you are not prepared for the battle, you will never win the war! And the more you run to counterfeit attempts like alcohol or other things to spot-repair something that needs completely overhauled, is like putting a patch over a patch. It may seem like a quick fix at the moment. But how has it actually changed your life for the better over this past year, or five years, or ten years? And how has it honestly affected your family's life over this time? We all need to change nearly everything about our lives!

When I look at my immediate family, I realize that—like the majority of people—we went through a lot as kids. We were very dysfunctional in many ways. My dad was a workaholic and an alcoholic. His approach was based on control. Control is a reaction to fear. Fear also affects our ability to learn, and to be creative. Search your heart today. Out of fear, do you stay partly angry at your spouse to get your own way? Back to control. Parents can do the same thing toward their children. This is not unusual at all.

Our mom went through a lot three-quarters of the time. It is really sad when I look back on it all. I found an outlet by running the streets. It was a poor decision, followed by many others.

After getting into trouble, I would walk to the local township building to face the music. On my way there, I would say to God, "If you get me out of this one, I will never do it again." Wink and a smile. He obviously was not fooled. Well, I didn't learn my lesson, and I found myself in family court. I was sentenced to eighteen months in a boy's home. From thirteen and a half years old until I was fifteen. The truth is, I didn't learn my lesson there either. I would go to church on Sundays. It was a requirement if you wanted to play on the basketball team. The problem was, I was more interested in the girl playing the piano than I was with what the pastor had to say.

Shortly after I returned home, I began to run the streets again. Consequently, my dad kicked me out of the house. I would steal food from the local grocery store and take baths at a nearby pond. Local police officers noticed I was sleeping in front of the school. They stopped to talk to me for a minute. Then they went to talk to my Aunt Marie and Uncle Ross. By the grace of God, they took me in for my junior and senior year in high school.

Aunt Marie was my dad's older sister. One of thirteen kids born on my grandparents' farm. She was totally old-school. As soon as I got home from school, playing sports, or work, she parked my butt at the kitchen table where I focused on my schoolwork. It paid off. I ended up on the honor roll and the merit roll a few times. I also bought a car and saved up two thousand dollars in the bank. After a year of having to be home before the streetlights came on, I decided to move back in with my parents. I went to a party one night with some friends. They picked me up and we went out to have some fun, or so we thought. After being out half the night, we headed back home. My friend was not driving well, so I took over. I didn't realize he had a headlight out, and I got pulled over. I ended up with three tickets. An insufficient driver's license. A broken headlight. And one for driving under the influence.

As crazy as it sounds at first, my Aunt and Uncle let me move back in with them (unconditional love). My Aunt made me sell my car to pay my fines, even though I had some money in the bank. It was clearly a way to teach me a lesson. I love you, Aunt Marie! Well, it was my senior year, and time to get busy again. I became the captain of the wrestling team. I loved playing sports. And I graduated with a business major. None of which would have happened without my Aunt Marie. It taught me that discipline and hard work pay off. From there, I traveled around the country quite a bit. I have been to Niagara Falls, the Adirondack Mountains, Washington, D.C., New York City, Florida, Texas, Arkansas, Oklahoma, Illinois, Ohio, and California. Then I went to tech school in Indiana to become a heavy equipment operator.

Our dad went through a lot as a child, too. So did our mom. They had six kids in six years (including a set of twins). You can see a clear generational pattern. The brokenness just continues down the line because we are not addressing these problems correctly. When we are born into this world, there is an unworldly innocence about us at first until we begin to have different experiences as a child and throughout our teenage years. Then we begin our lives as young adults.

[1] Man, who is born of woman,
Is short-lived and full of turmoil (Job 14:1 New American Standard Bible 1995).

So, what is the answer to all of this? How should

we live our lives? I believe we all need to learn how to love each other. How to forgive each other. How to serve one another by laying your life down for the good of others. This is all impossible without a personal relationship with God based on His Holy Word.

> [13] Greater love has no one than this, that one lay down his life for his friends (John 15:13 New American Standard Bible 1995).

God only knows what each one of us has gone through in our lives. As couples, we need to have a conversation about personal fears and insecurities. This should be part of everyone's premarital counseling, and as needed. What are the usual circumstances that trigger your fears to rise up?

In an effort to get to know each other a lot faster, make a list of the things you have in common. The things that you agree on. Then make a list of the things that you don't agree on. Then figure out what you can come together on, and what you can't. Seek wise counsel as needed. Then line up your differences with God's Word and pray for wisdom to make the changes you need to make in order to work together as a united team based on God's Holy Bible.

As you move forward in life, always

remember. Your spouse is not responsible for your pain, you are, which God is happy to resolve for you, if you are willing to let it go. If you were hurt as a child, it's not Christlike to pass that anger onto your spouse or children, or anyone else. That is not going to resolve your hurt and pain. Being judgmental, criticizing others, finding fault, being defensive. This is a very unhealthy way to live. Trust me. I've been there, done that, got the t-shirt. Try encouragement instead. It goes a long way.

Your spouse is actually a huge gift from God in your healing process if you go about it the correct way! Apply God's truth if you truly want to be free. The Goodness of God is truly amazing! Praise Him and thank Him every day that you have breath to do so.

> [3] Why do you look at the speck that is in your brother's eye, but do not notice
>
> the log that is in your own eye? [4] Or how can you say to your brother, 'Let me take the speck out of your eye,' and
>
> behold, the log is in your own eye? [5] You hypocrite, first take the log out of your own eye, and then you will see clearly to take the speck out of your brother's eye (Mattheew 7:3–5 New American Standard Bible 1995).

CHAPTER ELEVEN: WE ALL WANT TO LOVE AND BE LOVED

Agape love makes the world go around beautifully and graciously. And conditional love causes everything to fall flat quickly. A lack of love can cause a person to question whether they are accepted or not. It can cause you to feel uncomfortable. Sometimes you may feel insecure around certain people. Whether it is a family member, your spouse, your neighbor, a coworker, or someone else. This is universal—it doesn't matter if you are male or female. Or if you are black, white, blue, or green. It doesn't have anything to do with your age. It only matters how you personally communicate and demonstrate it to others, and whether it is genuine or not. It has everything to do with your heart.

One of the most interesting thoughts on the subject of love is how quickly things can change. We can love a family member one way during breakfast, and for whatever reason decide to treat them very differently during supper. Or you could be exchanging a cup of sugar with your neighbor all year, and the following year the only thing you share is a dislike for each other. Or you could have lunch with a coworker, and the following week they act distant toward you, or you toward them. That's the definition of conditional love. We've all been on the receiving end of it, and we've all been on the projecting end of it. But who of us only wants to be loved under certain conditions? And then knowing how it feels, why would we want to continue to be on the projecting end of it other than to control or hurt someone?

Like they say, hurt people hurt people. There is a lot of truth in that. We are all guilty of it. Either in a minor or major way. This is a much deeper issue that we all need to thoroughly examine no matter who we are, or what our role is. We simply cannot be serious about our walk with God and other relationships if we are not all-in on this in an effort to bring lasting healing, joy, and peace in all directions. People who are hurting filter every word or action taken through their past pain. When you hug someone who is hurting, it conveys a message that they are no longer *alone* in their pain!

> 23 Therefore if you are presenting your offering at the altar, and there remember that your brother has

something against you, [24] leave your offering there before the altar and go; first be reconciled to your brother, and then come and present your offering (Matthew 5:23–24).

God has commanded us to love our enemies as well. There is a world of difference between the way God loves us, and how we love each other!

[27] "But I say to you who hear, love your enemies, do good to those who hate you... (Luke 6:27 New American Standard Bible 1995).

Repeated acts of conditional love will naturally lead to feelings of rejection and abandonment. When those feelings are tied to those closest to us, it can trigger other unhealthy thoughts and feelings that we have all carried around for years. It's time to heal, and there is only one way to do that. Get rid of all the monkey business and stick to the truth, which is only found in God's Word.

Think back over this past year. How would your spouse, your children, your friends, and your neighbors describe in detail how you love each of them from one day to the next? Would they define it as being conditional or unconditional? Is your love consistent or inconsistent? Unforgiveness is directly tied to conditional love, and the number one reason for divorce. This shows us the serious negative impact it has on other relationships too, not just marriage. That's the very first thing God does for us when we ask. He forgives us, and never brings it up again. Truthfully, we do this to ourselves. That is why we stay stuck on first base. We have to get far more involved. We have to embrace all of God's design for healing and transformation, and it begins with forgiveness.

> [14] For if you forgive others for their transgressions, your heavenly Father will also forgive you (Matthew 6:14 New American Standard Bible 1995).

Pride is another stumbling block we have to overcome, which is also directly linked to unforgiveness. It is also the complete opposite of humility, which is one of the first steppingstones to great healing. Again, we are doing this to ourselves. It's time to do it God's way. The following verses give great insight on the issue:

> [33] The fear of the LORD is the instruction for wisdom,
> And before honor *comes* humility (Proverbs 15:33 New American Standard Bible 1995).

³ Do nothing from selfishness or empty conceit, but with humility of mind regard one another as more important than yourselves;

⁴ do not merely look out for your own personal interests, but also for the interests of others (Philippians 2:3–4 New American Standard Bible 1995).

² With all humility and gentleness, with patience, showing tolerance for one another in love, ³ being diligent to preserve the unity of the Spirit in the bond of peace (Ephesians 4:2–3 New American Standard Bible 1995).

We all have to search our hearts. *I mean truly examine what is going on deep down inside our souls.* Identify where unhealthy responses come from and why.

Defensiveness is another issue that can greatly affect our growth and maturity as Christians. Often, the urge is unholy in its origin. Perhaps you experienced harsh parenting, neglect, or abuse as a child that you have not overcome yet. Defensiveness arises from anything that feels like an attack on your character, lifestyle, decision making, or intelligence. It is usually accompanied by excuses.

I'm afraid that a lot of people just go through the motions every day but are not giving this the time and attention it deserves and requires. Once you have identified the real issues, you simply have to forgive others and move forward. It's very unhealthy and unproductive to remain in a state of unforgiveness. If you have decided to flat-out ignore problem areas in your life, how will you ever love and be loved? How will you ever have true peace in your heart? How will you ever experience true joy that overflows from an abiding life in Christ? You can't.

As adults we have the responsibility to be honest with ourselves by owning our sin against God and others. Don't miss this great opportunity God has given you to mature and become a great godly man or woman for His Glory!

> [11] When I was a child, I used to speak like a child, think like a child, reason like a child; when I became a man, I did away with childish things (1 Corinthians 13:11 New American Standard Bible 1995).

If we as married couples would spend more quality time coordinating our lives together, as well as studying together, we would naturally get along a lot better. After that, you simply apply Scripture in faith to every single issue that arises. Remember, you have to *replace* old ways of thinking and any hurt feelings, both past and present with God's truth found only in His Word. God did not complicate this! We are the ones complicating this whole process by not trusting Him fully and completely in the moment.

I would encourage you to take a journey back to your K-12 days. What was your home life like? Were both of your parents present growing up? Were they both engaged in your upbringing? Did you grow up in a healthy home overall, or was it dysfunctional? What was the main focus each week? Was there an emphasis on growing in your faith in Christ? In learning and applying God's Word? Did your parents help you process through things to help you better understand God and life, or did they discard God, and you were left to try to figure things out for yourself?

Did you do things together as a family unit? Maybe as a youth you became an avoider by staying in your bedroom half the time (Yerkovich & Yerkovich, 2009). Or maybe you became a people pleaser by trying to keep others happy as a way to cope with the dysfunction and uncertainty. Perhaps you became a controller to feel like you were in charge. Or maybe you became a vacillator because a loved one in your life rescheduled with you one too many times. Or perhaps you become a victim, and you just kept quiet (Yerkovich & Yerkovich, 2009).

Any kind or degree of childhood trauma necessitates looking back on your life to help you connect the dots.

Go back to the Fall of mankind and work your way forward. Just growing up in a sinful, fallen, cursed world affects us all terribly. There are solid reasons you live and behave like you do as an adult. And unless you biblically address what you are experiencing and why, you will never heal and mature in Christlikeness like you could have otherwise. Keep in mind, we experienced these things at a very young age. Our minds were not even fully developed yet.

Let's go back to your high school years for a minute. How did you spend your time? Did you engulf yourself in your studies? Did you play a lot of sports as a way to keep your mind busy? Maybe you hung out on the streets and partied with friends to replace your parents' absence. There are a lot of very unhealthy experiences we can go through depending on our situation. Ignoring reality will never eliminate the effects of negative childhood experiences from our adult life. There are no shortcuts to true healing. We have to address them correctly and directly in order to experience true change. Settling for less than God's best will only add to your regret. And trying to stay busy to avoid any thoughts or memories concerning all of this is just another lie from the devil. Becoming wise to how he operates is key to all of this!

Maybe you watch a lot of TV today or spend time on your phone as a way to keep your mind occupied on different things. Maybe you have tried to avoid a deeper conversation related to these subjects because of the cost to you personally. The bottom line is that Satan wants to keep you from doing it God's way, because that will lead you to true transformation as a Christian. We all have to ask ourselves, why wouldn't I want to experience God's best for my life?

Remember, we were all born with a sinful nature which eliminates anyone from being perfect at anything. We are all greatly flawed and in need of God's help. And where our parents did a great job, they deserve our great appreciation. Where they fell short or totally dropped the ball, they need our sincere forgiveness so families can heal, grow, and enjoy each other moving forward. Otherwise, we are just allowing Satan to deceive, divide, and destroy us without fighting back spiritually. And if you don't correct it, it just gets passed onto your children and grandchildren. Again, that's not a legacy you will be proud of down the road.

Parenting has to be an incredibly challenging job. My wife and I do not have children, but we can relate to a degree from our own experiences growing up. One thing that seems obvious is it would get better or worse depending on what each parent's environment was like when they themselves were being raised as a child. A person just can't do this properly without God's help and insight.

Good communication is a necessity. You can't function well if you can't effectively communicate with others. Only use words that are edifying. Be quick to use your manners to show respect and appreciation. Manipulation of any kind, sarcasm, passive-aggressive behavior, reverse psychology, and so-called little white lies are all part of the problem. It's critical we all see past this, and recognize we are being deceived every day we allow this stuff to continue. To do this correctly, we need to change nearly everything about our lives, which is completely doable with God's help. It's time to get after it!

[1] A gentle answer turns away wrath,
But a harsh word stirs up anger.

[2] The tongue of the wise makes knowledge acceptable,
But the mouth of fools spouts folly.

[3] The eyes of the Lord are in every place,
Watching the evil and the good.

[4] A soothing tongue is a tree of life,

But perversion in it crushes the spirit.

⁵ A fool rejects his father's discipline,
But he who regards reproof is sensible
(Proverbs 15:1–5 New American
Standard Bible 1995).

Have you ever personally experienced agape love? Yes, we've all experienced it coming from God. But have you learned much about it and intentionally applied it to your marriage and parenting? Have you modeled it to your spouse? Have you trained it into your children? Have you modeled it to your neighbors and others? Again, you have to love God's Word. Take a look with me:

¹⁶ "For God so loved the world, that He gave His only begotten Son, that whoever believes in Him shall not perish, but have eternal life (John 3:16 New American Standard Bible 1995).

²² But the fruit of the Spirit is love, joy, peace, patience, kindness, goodness, faithfulness, ²³ gentleness, self-control; against such things there is no law (Galatians 5:22–23 New American Standard Bible 1995).

²² Wives, be subject to your own

husbands, as to the Lord. [23] For the husband is the head of the wife, as Christ also is the Head of the Church, He Himself being the Savior of the body. [24] But as the Church is subject to Christ, so also the wives ought to be to their husbands in everything (Ephesians 5:22–24 New American Standard Bible 1995).

[25] Husbands, love your wives, just as Christ also loved the church and gave Himself up for her, [26] so that He might sanctify her, having cleansed her by the washing of water with the word (Ephesians 5:25–26 New American Standard Bible 1995).

[1] Children, obey your parents in the Lord, for this is right. [2] Honor your father and mother (which is the first commandment with a promise), [3] so that it may be well with you, and that you may live long on the earth. [4] Fathers, do not provoke your children to anger, but bring them up in the discipline and instruction of the Lord (Ephesians 6:1–4 New American

Standard Bible 1995).

⁷ For God has not given us a spirit of timidity, but of power and love and discipline (2 Timothy 1:7 New American Standard Bible 1995).

²⁷ And he answered, "You shall love the Lord your God with all your heart, and with all your soul, and with all your strength, and with all your mind; and your neighbor as yourself." (Luke 10:27 New American Standard Bible 1995).

¹⁸ There is no fear in love; but perfect love casts out fear, because fear involves punishment, and the one who fears is not perfected in love (1 John 4:18 New American Standard Bible 1995).

God is love and He longs to teach us everything about it. Love is what sent Christ to the Cross. He sure didn't do it because He was going to enjoy being tortured to death for the penalty of our sin. He did it because He was willing to give everything. That is amazing grace. He could have avoided the Cross just by sending us all to hell. Praise Him and thank Him for His incredible sacrifice so we can be forgiven of our sin and spend all eternity in Heaven with Him! Memorize, meditate on, and apply the four principles of agape love to your marriage, your precious children, and your neighbors. Agape love consists of the following:

1. God's love toward us is not dependent on our feelings toward Him.
2. God's love toward us is not dependent on our responses toward Him.
3. God's love toward us is not dependent on our past or present circumstances.
4. God's love toward us is not dependent on what we've done or haven't done for Him (Missler, 2009).

Think of all the wicked, ruthless things they did to Jesus. He was spit on, slapped, punched, whipped, and stabbed. Then they stuffed a crown of thorns down onto His head. When He pushed up from the spikes driven through His feet to try to relieve the pain in His hands, His feet screamed out even more. And when He lifted up with His hands to try to relieve some of the unimaginable pain in His feet, His hands writhed in agony. On top of that, they told all kinds of lies about Him that continue today. And yet, He didn't call down a legion of angels like you and I would have to wipe them all out. Instead, He humbled Himself and bore it all for our sake. Meditate on the verses below as a reminder of how we should be living out the rest of our lives while we have an opportunity to do so:

> [21] For you have been called for this purpose, since Christ also suffered for you, leaving you an example for you to follow in His steps, [22] who committed no sin, nor was any deceit found in His mouth; [23] and while being reviled, He did not revile in return; while suffering, He uttered no threats, but kept entrusting Himself to Him who judges righteously (1 Peter 2:21–23 New American Standard Bible 1995).

Husbands—and I'm preaching to myself here too —we could all do a lot more when it comes to dying to self to the degree that is required to fulfill our ministries. Consider how long you endure an uncomfortable situation before you get triggered. Compare what might be going through your heart and mind with Christ's example above. The next time you are in the heat of the moment, model Christ's love and grace for all the world to see— including to the little ones running around your house. Sure, we're going to blow it some days, but we can't give up. Keep growing in your faith. Bring Glory and Honor to God's name!

In 1 Peter above, it says, "He uttered no

threats." So, the next time you find yourself in the middle of an argument, be aware of comments such as, "You better stop." Notice the tone. That sounds like a threat. It sends a message to your brain that you've given them a warning. We have to be very wise when it comes to these types of situations. Sometimes you might think getting angry helps because anger is known as a separating emotion. But it is not going to help the growth of your marriage. It's wise to defuse at times during your healing process, but that is not what we're talking about here. That is just continuing to repeat what you have been doing.

Be honest. How would you describe your progress over the last few years? Are you pleased with the results? Would you give yourself an A, B, C, or D? The way we perceive our spouses can determine the way we treat them. As husbands, we have to remember that our wives' responses are a reflection of our daily affection toward them. The bottom line is, we all have a lot more to learn! Communicate that you care. Seek first to understand, then to be understood. Here's another great verse to meditate on every day:

> [18] In the exercise of His will He brought us forth by the word of truth, so that we would be a kind of first fruits among His creatures. [19] This you know, my beloved

brethren. But everyone must be quick to hear, slow to speak and slow to anger; [20] for the anger of man does not achieve the righteousness of God (James 1:18–20 New American Standard Bible 1995).

When we apply the four principles of agape love consistently, we open up a whole new door of understanding which leads to great healing and transformation. You experience God live in action right in front of you as you humbly submit and obey Him. Who doesn't want that? Who among us would say I would rather stay stuck where I am and be unhappy, unfulfilled, hurt, and without real hope for the rest of my life? Do you know why we stay stuck? Either because we don't have the right answers, or we are not applying the truth.

Everyone needs the kindness of our Savior and Lord who is Jesus Christ as an example for us to follow. Our motive and desire every day must be to love each other unconditionally! It is the only way to achieve true change. I challenge you to apply these four principles of agape love to every conversation you have and watch what happens. There's nothing left to argue about unless you're determined to stay stuck in a state of control, dysfunction, and loneliness. Why sacrifice precious love, joy, and peace every week? That's like going to the lake for some fun and it rains. Instead of being refreshed and enjoying some beautiful sunshine with precious loved ones, you miss out on what would have otherwise been a wonderful day. We are raining on our own parade year after year. It's high time to make the changes we all know we need to make.

Let's say your wife asked you to stop at the store on your way home, and you forgot. As you walk into the house, you can see she is starting to get upset. It's obvious you didn't stop at the store like she had asked, so she starts to express her feelings and emotions. On top of that, this isn't the first time you have forgotten to stop at the store. At that point, you're both feeling the weight of the moment, and now you have a decision to make. Do you want to continue to go down the same old road again, or do you want to hit the pause button and slow down? Think of it in terms of being a good defensive driver in order to avoid accidents. The first step is to slow down and pay close attention to detail.

In August of 2022, I turned fifty-nine. At the same time, I came across the Bible verse Matthew 5:9. One day I looked up at a digital clock in our bedroom, and it said 7:59 am. The 59 caught my attention because of my age, but then I thought of the Bible verse, and made another connection.

> [9] "Blessed are the peacemakers, for they shall be called sons of God (Matthew 5:9 New American Standard Bible 1995).

I'm a clock watcher, so I'm looking at the clock often throughout the day. Every time I see 59, I immediately quote that verse and acknowledge God, thanking Him for the reminder. It happens all the time now. It's very precious to me!

In great measure our lives equal the sum of our choices. It boils down to decision making. First of all, are you listening to the right voice in your head? Make sure you are being guided by the Holy Spirit. Remember, Satan will shoot thought bullets into your head to get you off track. Secondly, are you going to continue to build your marriage on the law? Are you yourselves trying to control the outcome of this process? At what point do we say enough is enough? I have to start doing things God's way and not my own. It can't be fifty percent of the time. It can't be ninety-five percent of the time either. It has to be an abiding life in Christ:

> [21] If righteousness comes through the Law, then Christ died needlessly (Galatians 2:21 New American Standard Bible 1995).

Meanwhile, your wife is still not happy with you for not stopping at the store. So, you say to yourself, "Because my love is not conditional, it is not dependent upon her feelings toward me, her responses toward me, our past or present circumstances, or what she has or hasn't done for me." One or more of these principles will apply to every situation in life. As your wife begins to catch herself because she's getting wise to Satan's lies, she will say to herself, "Because my love is not conditional, my love for my husband is not dependent upon his feelings toward me, his responses toward me, our past or present circumstances, or what he has or hasn't done for me."

This righteous approach destroys every misunderstanding, every disagreement, every argument, every lie from the enemy. There's nothing left for couples to do but to love each other *unconditionally*. To remain at peace, which brings glory to God and leads to a joy-filled evening. Who doesn't want that? Compare that to getting triggered, and away you go. Sound familiar? Instead of throwing pots and pans at each other, have a fun pillow fight instead. But keep in mind, you have to play by the rules. You can't sneak your pots and pans inside your pillowcase.

On a serious note: *we can never forget where your strength comes from.* It is not found in ourselves.

> [13] I can do all things through Him who strengthens me (Philippians 4:13 New

American Standard Bible 1995).

As a united team together, go on offense today. How do you go on the attack? Not by doing the same old thing. Feed your spirit ahead of time. Apply Scripture immediately, as if that is all you have ever done. Start to proactively prepare your heart and mind for the day before your feet hit the floor in the morning. Put on some praise and worship *every day*, and thank God for all that He has done for us, and for all that He is about to do!

Quality quiet time every day is a must. This is another example of why Scripture memory is so important. A good understanding of Scripture enables you to take the Word with you wherever you go.

When you're driving home from work or somewhere else, pull over in a safe place or in your driveway and meditate on them. If you're anticipating your spouse to return home in an hour, feed your spirit again. If you are caring for children, be creative. Pray for wisdom. Be mindful to take every thought captive to the obedience of Christ. It's far better to anticipate Satan's attacks and have your sword out and ready to go, than it is to try to pick up all the pieces afterword. Refuse to get deceived into the same old traps any longer. You can't just leave the door wide open and unattended! You have to guard and protect your household! Be determined to stand firm in your faith in Christ! This is spiritual warfare. Fight to win! The value of a soldier is not known in a time of peace, but in war. Think of Christ's example to us in the wilderness. Satan tried to deceive Him three times, and Jesus simply quoted Scripture to him, and told him to take a hike. The truth sets you free.

> [5] but if a man does not know how to manage his own household, how will he take care of the church of God? (1 Timothy 3:5 New American Standard Bible 1995).

> [9] And this I pray, that your love may abound still more and more in real knowledge and all discernment, [10] so that you may approve the things that are excellent, in order to be sincere and blameless until the day of Christ; [11] having been filled with the fruit of righteousness which comes through Jesus Christ, to the glory and praise of God (Philippians 1:9–11 New American Standard Bible).

Wisdom leads to maturity. Maturity does not come with age—it comes through submission and obedience to God's Word. Will you be controlled by the Holy Spirit if you're a born-again Christian, or will you continue to allow Satan to control you through different strongholds?

¹ Let not many of you become teachers, my brethren, knowing that as such we will incur a stricter judgment. ² For we all stumble in many ways. If anyone does not stumble in what he says, he is a perfect man, able to bridle the whole body as well. ³ Now if we put the bits into the horses' mouths so that they will obey us, we direct their entire body as well. ⁴ Look at the ships also, though they are so great and are driven by strong winds, are still directed by a very small rudder wherever the inclination of the pilot desires. ⁵ So also the tongue is a small part of the body, and yet it boasts of great things.

See how great a forest is set aflame by such a small fire! ⁶ And the tongue is a fire, the very world of iniquity; the tongue is set among our members as that which defiles the entire body, and sets on fire the course of our life, and is set on fire by hell. [7] For every species of beasts and birds, of reptiles and creatures of the sea, is tamed and has been tamed by the human race. [8] But no one can tame the tongue; it is a restless evil and full of deadly poison. [9] With it we bless our Lord and Father, and with it we curse men, who have been made in the likeness of God; [10] from the same mouth come both blessing and cursing. My brethren, these things ought not to be this way. [11] Does a fountain send out from the same opening both fresh and bitter water? [12] Can a fig tree, my brethren, produce olives, or a vine produce figs? Nor can salt water produce fresh.

[13] Who among you is wise and understanding? Let him show by his good behavior his deeds in the gentleness of wisdom. [14] But if you have bitter jealousy and selfish ambition in your heart, do not be arrogant and so lie against the truth. [15] This wisdom is not that which comes down from above, but is earthly, natural,

demonic. [16] For where jealousy and selfish ambition exist, there is disorder and every evil thing. [17] But the wisdom from above is first pure, then peaceable, gentle, reasonable, full of mercy and good fruits, unwavering, without hypocrisy. [18] And the seed whose fruit is righteousness is sown in peace by those who make peace. (James 3:1–18 New American Standard Bible 1995).

In hopes to encourage you to do the same, I'd like to pause right here for a minute and confess to you as I have to God many times. I have said unkind things to my wife Michelle in the middle of arguments. The Scriptures above are spot on, as always. Our tongues are evil and full of deadly poison. It's all a result of the Fall of Mankind. That does not give a person an excuse. We are still responsible for our actions. The good thing is, we don't have to stay there! Reach out to your spouse and ask for forgiveness and move on in faith as you heal, grow, and mature individually and as a couple.

[18] There is one who speaks rashly like the thrusts of a sword,
But the tongue of the wise brings healing (Proverbs 12:18 New American

Standard Bible).

It is very important we learn to slow down emotionally, physically, and spiritually so that we can discern things properly. Think of the acronym S.L.O.W. It stands for Stop, Listen, Obey, and Watch what God does. I actually bought four street signs and spread them around our house. The catch is, we don't get to watch what God will do in our lives if we don't do our part first—which is to stop, listen, and obey. When we as couples decide to respond in faith and submit and obey God rather than our flesh, great things happen. The point is, we all have a free will to think and to do as we wish. As a couple, agree to S.L.O.W. down, and watch what God will do to heal your hearts, minds, and marriage before your very eyes! If you haven't already experienced it, it's like no other. Once you get a taste of it, the feelings of doubt and fear you have carried all your life will begin to disappear. This is what real hope is made of, and it comes with a one hundred percent guarantee from a source you can count on, and that is God Himself. Give Him an opportunity—you won't be disappointed! I love the following verse:

> [22] But prove yourselves doers of the word, and not merely hearers who delude themselves (James 1:22 New American Standard Bible 1995).

I mentioned that there were two things that God put on my heart that, once better understood and applied, helped to heal our marriage enormously. It was agape love and spiritual warfare. These two topics turned out to be absolutely massive! Another *huge* matter God tried to point out to me again and again is the importance of "the two shall become one." Now there is the sexual aspect of this in terms of intimacy, but what we're talking about here reaches far beyond the physical element of marriage. We're talking about a precious unity together that covers every facet of a couple's lives over the course of their marriage. This happens when two lives unite and become one in purpose, heart, soul, and mind, and that is to bring Glory and Honor to God by fulfilling their ministry—all based on the Word of God!

> [24] For this reason a man shall leave his father and his mother, and be joined to his wife; and they shall become one flesh (Genesis 2:24 New American Standard Bible 1995).

As Christians, our responsibility is to follow Christ's lead, and love our wives as Christ loves the Church. He set aside His Godhead for us. Note to all husbands out there: it begins with us.

We are the head of our homes. Set aside your own wishes for your precious wife and her wellbeing. This means her spiritual wellbeing first and foremost, and then the rest of her needs in order to serve God fully and completely. This will position you for great success. Your wife's personal growth as a Christian is essential. Then they too are equipped for the ongoing battle that we will face every single day, for the rest of our lives.

This naturally enables your Christian beliefs to be passed on to your precious children to equip them for their teenage years and beyond. Time goes by fast. Do you remember the old saying, "Hold them while you can, they'll be walking soon,"? Then before you know it, they'll be going down the aisle in marriage. Then one evening while you're relaxing at home, you will receive a phone call informing you that you're soon to become grandparents. Incredible!

We need to come alongside our wives and assure them of our support in the same way Christ is always here for us, the true Church. A good habit to get into is to pray together and decide what your must-do's for the day and week are.

Don't forget, she is not only your wife, but she is one of God's daughters. The following verse assures us God will always do His part. So, live by faith and not by fear.

^{6} For I am confident of this very thing, that He who began a good work in you will perfect it until the day of Christ Jesus (Philippians 1:6 New American Standard Bible 1995).

Always remember, Satan will try to deceive you constantly. Learn to discern his lies quickly. What happens when someone does something nice for you? You want to bless them back, right? God assigned you the head of your home. He also assigned your wife to be your helpmate. God's design and intent for everything is always perfect. He always gives us the very best. All we have to do is *believe*. And I don't mean just to believe when everything seems to be perfect. I mean, believe even when the sky appears to be falling. Much like when God parted the Red Sea for Moses. God honored his faith. Praise God for the following blessings:

> ^{18} Then the Lord God said, "It is not good for the man to be alone; I will make him a helper suitable for him." (Genesis 2:18 New American Standard Bible 1995).

> ^{22} He who finds a wife finds a good thing, and obtains favor from the Lord (Proverbs 18:22 New American

Standard Bible 1995).

If you have been stuck for some time and feel like you're at your wits end, and you're not sure where to turn, *turn to Jesus*. It's not that it's impossible to fix your marriage; it is just a matter of how you are going about it. If you are married, you have to learn to work together as one united front to overcome this incredible battle. There is no other way. If we as husbands would care for our wives like we are commanded, our wives would return the favor tenfold. And the love, joy, and peace that comes from our obedience to God will bring great healing to our marriages and families. It will also give breath to our testimonies to share hope and encouragement to others. The following verse is a clear warning to us all:

> [5] Stop depriving one another, except by agreement for a time, so that you may devote yourselves to prayer, and come together again so that Satan will not tempt you because of your lack of self-control (1 Corinthians 7:5 New American Standard Bible 1995).

It's very important that we all learn from our mistakes. This is where humility and forgiveness come in.

When it comes to true intimacy, there is

a massive difference between spending quality time together, and just going for another quick roll in the hay. There is an opportunity for every husband and wife to experience great healing during times of intimacy. Rebuilding overall trust in our lives is one of them. This is very important because trust is at the root of all our unhealthy fears. It is also directly connected to past wounds and the pain associated with them. If we don't intentionally seek the correct kind of healing, we'll never break free from the bondage of strongholds. That would be like taking a pill every day that causes you great hurt and pain when you could easily trade it for a bowl of your favorite ice cream.

Sex without a wedding band, and sex without a heart of love, care, compassion, sensitivity, as well as personal warmth and gentleness toward your spouse is just sex. This reduces the act to pure lust for selfish reasons. That's not how God designed it. Void of a genuine caring heart, and a desire to serve your spouse, along with a correct vision and purpose for your marriage, couples are left to drift through life mostly frustrated and confused. Then our marriages become cheap imitations of what they should be, depending on the value and vision you endorse as a couple. Yes, there is a great deal more to life, and fulfilling your ministry together with your precious wife is at the very top of the list.

In January, 2012, my wife and I were really struggling. I remember thinking to myself on several occasions, "I don't know how this is ever going to work." We loved each other, but we were really struggling to put it all together.

Years ago, we said that, when we pass away, my gravestone is going to read, "I should have checked references," and Michelle's gravestone is going to say, "I should have kept looking." Humor is a necessity. All kidding aside, marriage is an investment that we cannot afford to miss. It was then that we decided that one of the many changes that we needed to make was to be much more intentional about our date days. Well, to make a long story short, we turned our living room into a dance floor, and if you don't mind me saying, other than a few toe surgeries, we're pretty good! It's a lot like ice skating, except it's on wheels. What better way to lead into our date day together? What a wonderful blessing for our marriage. Praise the Lord!

Another thing we did to add more fun to our date days was to mix things up. I bought my wife several different wigs. Some weeks I would pick a certain wig, and other weeks she would surprise me. Prior to starting our date day, I drive over to her door, and we pray and ask God to bless our time together. Then I move back away from the door with my eyes closed, and she'll walk out on the dance floor. Cowabunga, baby! Creativity is important!

A marriage relationship is meant to bond a husband and his wife together to become one in heart, soul, mind, and body. To cultivate, to nurture, to promote, to encourage, to foster, to support, to protect, and to minister to one another. All of this and more in a close and intimate way throughout their lifetime together:

> 3 Do nothing from selfishness or empty conceit, but with humility of mind regard one another as more important than yourselves;
>
> 4 do not merely look out for your own personal interests, but also for the interests of others (Philippians 2:3–4 New American Standard Bible 1995).

Often, if we would just change our perspective on things, we would be much better off. For example, think of the times you have gotten frustrated with your spouse or child for different reasons. We get frustrated because we don't like how their actions are affecting us personally or in other ways. But if we would learn to view it as a gift from God to help us grow personally, then what's the problem? *Growing in Christlikeness should be number one in our lives.*

Imagine if you were called up into heaven to

meet God in person and returned to earth with a whole new game plan. Would that not rock your world like no other? You would be all business for the rest of your life as you served the Lord one thousand percent! Depending on where you're at in your walk with God today, you may need to get a lot more involved. Join a good Bible study group on the subject of marriage. There are some good websites out there. Get some good study materials for yourself. Build a library. Memorize Scripture. Memorize key phrases that speak to your heart, too. You will also need a nightly accountability partner. This will speed up your growth and keep you on a straight and narrow path. Boundaries, discipline, and consistency are crucial!

Be very honest before God, yourself, and others. Humility is a great thing! Remember, God has given us the ability to do what is needed!

> [18] Poverty and shame will come to him who neglects discipline, but he who regards reproof will be honored (Proverbs 13:18 New American Standard Bible 1995).

This life tends to throw us curve balls when we're not expecting it. Things can be one way for a long time, and then *boom*—everything changes. Have you ever thought to yourself, what if I was to leave this world before my bride? Have I positioned her spiritually, relationally, financially, not to mention a hundred other things? These are the kind of questions we really need to be asking ourselves so we can prepare. Not to mention your children, and their precious lives. Are they prepared to meet their Maker? We all have a great responsibility, and if we are wise, we will err on the side of safety, and go the extra mile while we're in a position to do so. Time to raise the bar again and again for God's Glory and Honor!

> [4] Love is patient, love is kind and is not jealous; love does not brag and is not arrogant, [5] does not act unbecomingly; it does not seek its own, is not provoked, does not take into account a wrong suffered, [6] does not rejoice in unrighteousness, but rejoices with the truth; [7] bears all things, believes all things, hopes all things, endures all things (1 Corinthians 13:4–7 New American Standard Bible 1995).

CHAPTER TWELVE: FULFILLING YOUR MINISTRY

As Christians, we must be doers of the Word. We have a call to answer—we're either all in, or we're not. So, where do you stand? If your doctor instructed you to follow a strict diet, you would know in your heart-of-hearts whether you were following it to the letter or not. How about God's Word? Are you following it to the letter, or are you continuing to ignore certain things to accommodate the sin in your life? People are setting themselves up for *unimaginable regret* one day if they—for even one second—think that they're going to pull one over on God.

> [11] And He gave some as apostles, and some as prophets, and some as evangelists, and some as pastors and teachers, [12] for the equipping of the saints for the work of service, to the building up of the body of Christ; [13]

until we all attain to the unity of the faith, and of the knowledge of the Son of God, to a mature man, to the measure of the stature which belongs to the fullness of Christ. [14] As a result, we are no longer to be children, tossed here and there by waves and carried about by every wind of doctrine, by the trickery of men, by craftiness in deceitful scheming; [15] but speaking the truth in love, we are to grow up in all aspects into Him who is the head, even Christ, [16] from whom the whole body, being fitted and held together by what every joint supplies, according to the proper working of each individual part, causes the growth of the body for the building up of itself in love (Ephesians 4:11–16 New American Standard Bible 1995).

Aren't you glad Jesus is all in for us, the true Church? Imagine if God only thought about Himself. He would never have gone to the Cross. Where would that leave us today? Completely without hope and purpose. Doomed to hell for all eternity. Can you imagine such a fate? We the Church need to wise up and rise up and be the salt and the light on this earth. We need to get very serious about God's calling on our lives. Stop living from day-to-day. *Look at it from an eternal perspective.*

To be doers of the Word, we need to know God's Word first, so we can apply it correctly and immediately. I say this to encourage you to do the same. In 2013, I began to memorize Scripture. I will soon have memorized a total of one hundred and fifty Bible verses. Praise God! Each week I quote them to myself, as well as meditate on them and apply them accordingly. I came to a place in my life and walk with God where I needed God's Word written on my heart and mind. I am so grateful for the immediate access. I published a booklet with all of them categorized for easy access to help you and others.

When you think of Satan, spiritual warfare, strongholds—or when your flesh starts to rise up —it's right there at your fingertips. God could have given us a trillion different things. Instead, He gave us His Word, the Holy Bible, to read and to learn from. The infallible, inerrant Word of God. It is the key to our peace, wisdom, and freedom.

Again, remember Jesus' example to us in the wilderness when Satan was attacking Him. He was attacking His loyalty to God the Father, first and foremost. Nothing has changed.

What happens when we fail to apply God's Word when we're being attacked? We fail to trust God. Either we lack the understanding and discernment of what's actually going on in the background, or maybe we lack the patience and fortitude necessary to work through the process that healing and growing requires. Think about the dynamics of what you are working against. This is a very serious battle. It's not easy by any means. That's why we all make mistakes during this whole process. But we can't accept a lower standard. We have to be determined to win for God's Glory and Honor! Satan be damned to hell where he belongs! He has destroyed many, many lives. Don't add your name to the list. Guard and protect your precious family!

When we are going through difficult times, part of the problem is that we might stick it out for a short period of time before we respond out of our flesh. Notice how Satan tempted Jesus three times before he gave up. That means we too have to be prepared to persevere for as long as it takes. In doing so, we are retraining our hearts and minds. The result is Christlikeness, a healed marriage, a transformed heart, and a renewed mind. What's more, you will be a great example to precious children and others who are watching how you respond. True peace is powerful. The same peace that Jesus mentioned when He said, "My peace I give to you..." (John 14:27 New American Standard Bible). Who doesn't want that? Meditate on the following verse every day:

⁵ But you, be sober in all things, endure hardship, do the work of an evangelist, fulfill your ministry (2 Timothy 4:5 New American Standard Bible 1995).

If you know more about TV programs, sports, or the markets today than you do about God's Word, you need to reprioritize your to-do list. As husbands, we have been given the responsibility to give up everything for the wellbeing of our wives. This can only happen by strictly obeying God's Word.

We are to love our wives in a supportive, sacrificial, selfless, unreserved way every day, and let the Holy Spirit take care of the rest. This is not easy. Some days are harder than others. We're talking about transforming two broken lives into one Righteous life in the likeness of Christ. Spiritual discernment is the key here.

When we think of maturing in Christlikeness, the approach is not to eliminate or avoid all difficult situations in life. It's to respond in a correct manner while we're in the heat of the moment. By doing so, we are modeling peace and understanding to the situation. One of the big mistakes I've made over the years was buying into Satan's lie that things would never change. I needed to learn a whole lot more about the bigger picture that we all face. The following is another great passage to memorize:

> [7] Do not be deceived, God is not mocked; for whatever a man sows, this he will also reap. [8] For the one who sows to his own flesh will from the flesh reap corruption, but the one who sows to the Spirit will from the Spirit reap eternal life. [9] Let us not lose heart in doing good, for in due time we will reap if we do not grow weary. [10] So then, while we have opportunity, let us do good to all people, and especially to those who are of the household of the faith (Galatians 6:7–10 New American Standard Bible 1995).

Like I've mentioned a few times now, it is extremely important that we all get wise to Satan's schemes. They are designed to cause us to fail at bringing God glory. To fail as a husband, wife, dad, and mom. To fail as sons and daughters. As aunts and uncles. As grandmas and grandpas. And as a loving neighbor. Ultimately, he wants us to fail to fulfill our ministry as Christians. Understand, you are unique in God's eyes, and He has an exclusive ministry for you to accomplish. The Christian's life is meant to present Jesus Christ to a lost and dying world. Your faith goes wherever you go. Some people are not going to want to hear it. That is their decision.

> [14] Whoever does not receive you, nor heed your words, as you go out of that house or that city, shake the dust off your feet. [15] Truly I say to you, it will be more tolerable for the land of Sodom and Gomorrah in the day of judgment than for that city (Matthew 10:14–15 New American Standard Bible 1995).

We have to keep pressing on! We all have a specific role to play. A story to tell. Keep your eyes fixed on God! Sharing and modeling the love of Christ with others is wonderful knowing you are giving them the truth that can set them free once and for all. What a blessing to be a part of God's family and Kingdom! Is there a greater calling in all of life?

Notice what happens to us when we take our eye off the Lord. Peter became fearful and focused his attention on the wind instead of God's Word. The result was he began to sink, and that's exactly what happens to us when we act out of fear, is it not? And just like our Lord helps us every day, He saved Peter's life. Doubting God has never gotten us anywhere, and it never will. Trusting Him, however, will calm storms, part seas, and move mountains.

^{28} Peter said to Him, "Lord, if it is You, command me to come to You on the water." ^{29} And He said, "Come!" And Peter got out of the boat, and walked on the water and came toward Jesus. ^{30} But seeing the wind, he became frightened, and beginning to sink, he cried out, "Lord, save me!" ^{31} Immediately Jesus stretched out His hand and took hold of him, and said to him, "You of little faith, why did you doubt?" ^{32} When they got into the boat, the wind stopped. ^{33} And those who were in the boat worshiped Him, saying, "You are certainly God's Son!" (Matthew 14:28–33 New American Standard Bible).

We have all struggled with our faith at times. It is all part of us maturing as Christians. Peter took his eyes off the Lord and focused on the wind. Doubting Thomas said he would have to "see with his own eyes" before he would believe.

^{24} But Thomas, one of the twelve, called Didymus, was not with them when Jesus came.

^{25} So the other disciples were saying to

him, "We have seen the Lord!" But he said to them, "Unless I see in His hands the imprint of the nails, and put my finger into the place of the nails, and put my hand into His side, I will not believe."

26 After eight days His disciples were again inside, and Thomas with them. Jesus came, the doors having been shut, and stood in their midst and said, "Peace be with you."

27 Then He said to Thomas, "Reach here with your finger, and see My hands; and reach here your hand and put it into My side; and do not be unbelieving, but believing."

28 Thomas answered and said to Him, "My Lord and my God!"

29 Jesus said to him, "Because you have seen Me, have you believed? Blessed are they who did not see, and yet believed." (John 20:24–29 New American Standard Bible 1995).

7 for we walk by faith, not by sight — (2 Corinthians 5:7 New American Standard Bible 1995).

6 And without faith it is impossible to

please Him, for he who comes to God must believe that He is and that He is a rewarder of those who seek Him (Hebrews 11:6 New American Standard Bible 1995).

[11] Now faith is the assurance of things hoped for, the conviction of things not seen (Hebrews 11:1 New American Standard Bible 1995).

Exercising your faith, and fulfilling your ministry first starts at home. As husbands, we are the head of our household. If you are not already a strong leader, or becoming one, you need to do so right away. Simply follow Christ's example. That's what His life was all about. Pass on what you learn to your wife so you can become what I call a S.W.A.T. team together. The idea of a S.W.A.T. team is for husbands and wives to work together in such a way that they have each other's back. You come to each other's rescue. I'm talking about *spiritual warfare*! So, you should be *proactively* on guard against the enemy who is out to destroy you and your family. It's high time we as the body of Christ go on offense by exercising our faith instead of doubting God and being on defense all the time. A strong offense is a good defense. Open up God's Holy Word and apply it as He intended for us to do!

The acronym S.W.A.T. stands for Satan Will Attack Today. Say to yourselves, "It's us against them," meaning it is God, you, and your wife against Satan and his cohorts. Then say to yourself, "Not on my watch!" Stand your ground. Be intentional to fight to protect your marriage and children. If we don't get wise to what all is going on in the spiritual realm, and how it affects us here on earth personally, we will remain clueless when it comes to attaining victory over this very real and serious battle.

As I mentioned before, Satan tries to hold us hostage through strongholds that he sets up in our minds as children. The more you train and prepare as a couple, the greater your safety and unity will be. If you start going off track, stop immediately and pray. Start quoting Scripture. Believe wholeheartedly that God has gone before you because He has! Exercise your faith. Put on the Full Armor of God and leave it on. Stand firm and say, "I refuse to allow this to happen to our marriage any longer. I refuse to allow these lies, deceptions, and schemes to affect our family and household again today." Pray and ask God to destroy all strongholds affecting you and your family. Open your front door and tell Satan to take a hike!

Recently, I put a tall markerboard on wheels in our bedroom with Bible verses on it to keep God's Word right in front of us. During the day, we position it in our living room. It's been a great blessing! I encourage you to do the same. We also have a few slow-down signs, some S.W.A.T. hats, and a couple "What Would Jesus Do" printouts. It's similar in a way to hanging a Cross on your wall. It's a reminder of the great sacrifice Christ paid for our sins. It also illustrates the length that He was willing to go for us. Now, the question is, to what length are we willing to go for Him?

Look at these visuals as helpful tools as we transform our awareness to include the spiritual realm as well! This is crucial if we as Christians are to overcome all of the enemies' attacks. Then when someone visits your home, you can share with them the understanding behind such objects, along with the Gospel.

Remember, Satan was defeated at the Cross. The only influence he has in our lives is what we allow. He needs a vehicle to work through. How many times have you become a vehicle for the devil over the past year? What have you learned from it? How have things changed for the better in the last month? Once you decide to take a stand based on God's Word, the acronym for S.W.A.T. becomes *Satan Was All Talk.*

[1] I solemnly charge you in the presence of God and of Christ Jesus, who is to judge the living and the dead, and by His

appearing and His kingdom: [2] preach the word; be ready in season and out of season; reprove, rebuke, exhort, with great patience and instruction. [3] For the time will come when they will not endure sound doctrine; but wanting to have their ears tickled, they will accumulate for themselves teachers in accordance to their own desires, [4] and will turn away their ears from the truth and will turn aside to myths. [5] But you, be sober in all things, endure hardship, do the work of an evangelist, fulfill your ministry (2 Timothy 4:1–5 New American Standard Bible 1995).

Did you catch that? People will just want their ears tickled. They will accumulate for themselves teachers in accordance with their own desires. This is the concern. We're being deceived by the enemy, which will result in our own demise if we're not careful. On the other hand, wouldn't it be wonderful to grow more and more in Christlikeness every day? That means we have to give up anything and everything that is standing in the way. We cannot afford to return to first base when we should be standing on second or third base as we pursue wisdom derived from God's Word that, when applied, will enable us to overcome.

> ¹² For though by this time you ought to be teachers, you have need again for someone to teach you the elementary principles of the oracles of God, and you have come to need milk and not solid food. ¹³ For everyone who partakes only of milk is not accustomed to the word of righteousness, for he is an infant. ¹⁴ But solid food is for the mature, who because of practice have their senses trained to discern good and evil (Hebrews 5:12–14 New American Standard Bible 1995).

Fulfilling your ministry is going to require unwavering faith, daily discipline, and perseverance until Christ's return. A prayer offered up in faith will move mountains. Prayer opens the door between God and His children. From there a personal, intimate relationship is born, and great healing and transformation begins as we grow in Christlikeness. As you can see below, Jesus is very serious about all this, as we should be.

> ⁶² But Jesus said to him, "No one, after putting his hand to the plow and

looking back, is fit for the kingdom of God." (Luke 9:62 New American Standard Bible 1995).

We need to be praying every day, all day, at every turn, at every bump in the road. Pray in faith, not in fear. Can you imagine hearing someone verbally end their prayer by saying, "I pray in fear in Jesus' name, Amen,"?

Prayer is how we communicate and have fellowship with God Himself—which is amazing. Your prayers can be audible or silent, public or private. We are seeking God's favor. We are seeking His will, and not ours. God wants us to talk to Him about everything. Through prayer we develop a personal relationship with Him. This is how we build trust. When we pray, we express our love and appreciation for all that God has done for us. We thank Him and tell Him how much we truly love Him. Through prayer we are seeking to align our will with God's will. God's House must be a House of prayer, and God's people must be people of prayer as we seek to honor Him in every way! Modeling His likeness is of paramount importance.

As the body of Christ, let's start relocating some mountains—beginning with the one right in front of us—so we can fulfill our ministry for God's Glory! Post the following verse on your markerboard or in your bathroom as another daily reminder:

> [20] And He said to them, "Because of the littleness of your faith; for truly I say to you, if you have faith the size of a mustard seed, you will say to this mountain, 'Move from here to there,' and it will move; and nothing will be impossible to you (Matthew 17:20 New American Standard Bible 1995).

God honors our faith. He promises to take care of all our needs. If we are about God's business, He will be about our business. The opposite is also true. If we do not stay focused on doing God's will, then we have knowingly and intentionally shifted our focus back to ourselves; right where Satan wants us. Again, if you are married, you will continue to argue over different things because you are not moving in the same direction together as followers of Jesus Christ. We can fall into old habits of wanting our own way, and we stay stuck there. Your wife at one end of the house, and you the husband at the other end. Christ is the only bridge between the kitchen and the den.

> [1] What is the source of quarrels and conflicts among you? Is not the source your pleasures that wage war in your

members? ² You lust and do not have; so you commit murder. You are envious and cannot obtain; so you fight and quarrel. You do not have because you do not ask. ³ You ask and do not receive, because you ask with wrong motives, so that you may spend it on your pleasures (James 4:1–3 New American Standard Bible 1995).

When we say to ourselves, "There's got to be more to life than this," what are we actually saying? We are pointing to a void in our lives that we have been unable or unwilling to fill. Not to mention any unhealed experiences you've gone through that have not been addressed correctly.

If you had a choice between receiving a million dollars and a life on earth, or to go straight to heaven without a dime, which would you choose? Search your heart. Do you long to meet your Lord and Savior? Do you long to enter Heaven to worship, praise, and thank our Lord for everything He has done for us? Or do you long to climb the ladder at work, and find for yourself things to help you become more comfortable in this life?

If you are a young person today, don't lose hope. Live by faith, not by sight. Instead, be very careful who you are listening to. This life isn't all there is. If your faith is in Jesus Christ alone, you have a lot to look forward to. Get excited! Be an example to others. Don't just go along to get along. Be willing to be different. Heaven is for all eternity!

> ¹⁸ For I consider that the sufferings of this present time are not worthy to be compared with the glory that is to be revealed to us (Romans 8:18 New American Standard Bible 1995).

> ¹² Not that I have already obtained it or have already become perfect, but I press on so that I may lay hold of that for which also I was laid hold of by Christ Jesus. ¹³ Brethren, I do not regard myself as having laid hold of it yet; but one thing I do: forgetting what lies behind and reaching forward to what lies ahead, ¹⁴ I press on toward the goal for the prize of the upward call of God in Christ Jesus (Philippians 3:12–14 New American Standard Bible 1995).

If you are an elderly person today, you still have more work to do. It isn't over until it's over. As long as you have breath in you, preach the Word! Maybe it's a nurse, doctor, or therapist alongside your bed. Pour into every person you meet. Leave it all on the field. Everyone benefits from your knowledge and experience. We need sound teachers today.

The Ten Commandments clearly demonstrate to us that we have all sinned and fall short of the Glory of God. When you read down through this passage, keep score to see where you stand. Be very honest before God. He already knows the truth! Then envision the day and the hour you will meet God face to face. Will you be humble and excited at the same time for everything you did for God's name's sake, or will you have missed the boat? God is going to separate the sheep from the goats. What line will you be standing in?

The Ten Commandments

[1] Then God spoke all these words, saying,

[2] "I am the Lord your God, who brought you out of the land of Egypt, out of the house of slavery.

[3] "You shall have no other gods before Me.

[4] "You shall not make for yourself an idol, or any likeness of what is in heaven above or on the earth beneath or in the water under the earth. [5] You shall

not worship them or serve them; for I, the Lord your God, am a jealous God, visiting the iniquity of the fathers on the children, on the third and the fourth generations of those who hate Me, [6] but showing lovingkindness to thousands, to those who love Me and keep My commandments.

[7] "You shall not take the name of the Lord your God in vain, for the Lord will not leave him unpunished who takes His name in vain.

[8] "Remember the sabbath day, to keep it holy. [9] Six days you shall labor and do all your work, [10] but the seventh day is a sabbath of the Lord your God; in it you shall not do any work, you or your son or your daughter, your male or your female servant or your cattle or your sojourner who stays with you. [11] For in six days the Lord made the heavens and the earth, the sea and all that is in them, and rested on the seventh day; therefore the Lord blessed the sabbath day and made it holy.

[12] "Honor your father and your mother, that your days may be prolonged in the land which the Lord your God gives you.

[13] "You shall not murder.

[14] "You shall not commit adultery.

[15] "You shall not steal.

[16] "You shall not bear false witness against your neighbor.

[17] "You shall not covet your neighbor's house; you shall not covet your neighbor's wife or his male servant or his female servant or his ox or his donkey or anything that belongs to your neighbor." (Exodus 20:1–17 New American Standard Bible).

Imagine, everything you have ever said or done will be out in the open. No more little secrets. God is going to clean house. Repent now and turn in the opposite direction. Meditate long and hard on the following verses (I mentioned this passage earlier, but some things are worth repeating).

[2] But there is nothing covered up that will not be revealed, and hidden that will not be known. [3] Accordingly, whatever you have said in the dark will be heard in the light, and what you have whispered in the inner rooms will be proclaimed upon the housetops.

[4] "I say to you, My friends, do not be

afraid of those who kill the body and after that have no more that they can

do. [5] But I will warn you whom to fear: fear the One who, after He has killed, has authority to cast into hell; yes, I tell you, fear Him! (Luke 12:2–5 New American Standard Bible 1995).

Life has taught me many lessons over the years. The biggest one is that trials are a good thing. They take us where we would not otherwise want to go. And through these experiences, we learn how dependent we are on God. And when you learn to trust God in everything, you will never see the world the same, and you will never spend another moment alone or without hope. He will always walk alongside you every step of the way! Remember, you have everything to gain, and nothing to lose.

Open up your Bible every day and develop a personal relationship with God. Teach your family to pray and trust God in every circumstance by your own example. Share the Gospel with your family. Disciple them. Become true followers of Jesus Christ. Get grounded and become the person God desires you to be. Put aside the foolishness of this world. A Bible-based Church will help you on this journey. Jesus Christ is soon to return for His children. The Bible tells us, He's coming for those who are looking for

Him.

If my mom, who died very unexpectedly, is in Heaven today, it's because she prayed a prayer of repentance at the end of a Church service she was watching near the end of her life. Like I said, when things happen in our lives, they often take us by surprise. Tomorrow is not a guarantee. *Nobody* is exempt.

> [21] He made Him who knew no sin to be sin on our behalf, so that we might become the righteousness of God in Him (2 Corinthians 5:21 New American Standard Bible 1995).

> [6] Jesus said to him, "I am the way, and the truth, and the life; no one comes to the Father but through Me (John 14: 6 New American Standard Bible 1995).

> [9] That if you confess with your mouth Jesus as Lord,
> and believe in your heart that God raised Him from the dead, you will be saved;
> [10] for with the heart a person believes, resulting in righteousness,
> and with the mouth he confesses, resulting in salvation (Romans 10:9–10 New American Standard Bible 1995).

[38] Peter said to them, "Repent, and each of you be baptized in the name of Jesus Christ for the forgiveness of your sins; and you will receive the gift of the Holy Spirit (Acts 2:38. New American Standard Bible 1995).

[10] so that at the name of Jesus every knee will bow, of those who are in heaven and on earth and under the earth, [11] and that every tongue will confess that Jesus Christ is Lord, to the glory of God the Father (Philippians 2:10–11 New American Standard Bible 1995).

[13] I am the Alpha and the Omega, the first and the last, the beginning and the end."

[14] Blessed are those who wash their robes, so that they may have the right to the tree of life, and may enter by the gates into the city. [15] Outside are the dogs and the sorcerers and the immoral persons and the murderers and the idolaters, and everyone who loves and practices lying (Revelation 22:13–15 New American Standard Bible 1995).

[16] "Behold, I send you out as sheep in the midst of wolves; so be shrewd as serpents and innocent as doves (Matthew 10:16 New American Standard Bible 1995).

[58] Therefore, my beloved brethren, be steadfast, immovable, always abounding in the work of the Lord, knowing that your toil is not *in* vain in the Lord (1 Corinthians 15:58 New American Standard Bible 1995).

[22] Strengthening the souls of the disciples, encouraging them to continue in the faith, and *saying*, "Through many tribulations we must enter the kingdom of God." (Acts 14:22 New American Standard Bible 1995).

[8] We are afflicted in every way, but not crushed; perplexed, but not despairing;

[9] persecuted, but not forsaken; struck down, but not destroyed (2 Corinthians 4:8–9 New American Standard Bible 1995).

[16] Therefore we do not lose heart, but though our outer man is decaying, yet

our inner man is being renewed day by day.

17 For momentary, light affliction is producing for us an eternal weight of glory far beyond all comparison,

18 while we look not at the things which are seen, but at the things which are not seen; for the things which are seen are temporal, but the things which are not seen are eternal (2 Corinthians 4:16–18).

4 You are from God, little children, and have overcome them; because greater is He who is in you than he who is in the world (1 John 4:4 New American Standard Bible 1995).

Jesus has been labeled the bad guy for two-thousand-plus years. We the body of Christ need to Honor our Lord by following the example that He modeled to us! We need to fully obey what has been taught to us in God's Holy Word. We are either going to glorify God by our obedience to His Word, or we are going to glorify Satan in our rebellion against God. God has given us all a free will. The ball is in your court. This is the first day of the rest of your life!

11 "Blessed are you when people insult

you and persecute you, and falsely say all kinds of evil against you because of Me (Matthew 5:11 New American Standard Bible 1995).

CHAPTER THIRTEEN: FOR ALL ETERNITY

Our lives as we know it are about to come to an end! Please carefully consider everything that you've read so far, and what you're about to read. This has everlasting consequences. Bible prophecy describes God's plans for the future. Let's take a look at where we are, and what's to come.

> ^{18} I also say to you that you are Peter, and upon this rock I will build My church; and the gates of Hades will not overpower it (Matthew 16:18 New American Standard Bible 1995).

The Church Age. The first event in Bible prophecy is the Church Age. It's the period of time from Pentecost to the Rapture. It's known as the Church Age because it covers the time in which the Church is on the earth.

God issued an invitation to Abraham and his descendants, the Jews, to be in a covenant relationship with Him. But Israel decided to temporarily reject that invitation when they rejected Christ. So, God extended His invitation to the Gentiles that we might be saved, which is where we are today.

> [11] I say then, God has not rejected His people, has He? May it never be! For I too am an Israelite, a descendant of Abraham, of the tribe of Benjamin (Romans 11:1 New American Standard Bible 1995).

> [25] For I do not want you, brethren, to be uninformed of this mystery—so that you will not be wise in your own estimation—that a partial hardening has happened to Israel until the fullness of the Gentiles has come in (Romans 11:25 New American Standard Bible 1995).

When you think of the Church, don't think of a building or different denominations. The Church itself is universal, but it meets within smaller bodies in local communities.

Think of individuals who have placed their faith in Jesus Christ as their Lord and Savior for their Salvation. Think of it as the Body of Christ at large, of which He is the Head.

^{12} But as many as received Him, to them He gave the right to become children of God, even to those who believe in His name (John 1:12 New American Standard Bible 1995).

^{31} So the church throughout all Judea and Galilee and Samaria enjoyed peace, being built up; and going on in the fear of the Lord and in the comfort of the Holy Spirit, it continued to increase (Acts 9:31 New American Standard Bible 1995).

^{22} And He put all things in subjection under His feet, and gave Him as head over all things to the church, ^{23} which is His body, the fullness of Him who fills all in all (Ephesians 1:22–23 New American Standard Bible 1995).

The Church Age corresponds with the dispensation of God's Grace toward mankind. We were given the law through Moses, and grace and truth came through Jesus Christ. The Church Age is marked by the Holy Spirit permanently and eternally indwelling believers who have placed their faith and trust in Christ for their Salvation.

¹⁶ I will ask the Father, and He will give you another Helper, that He may be with you forever (John 14:16 New American Standard Bible 1995).

The Bible makes a distinction between the nation of Israel and the Church. But there is also some overlap because many Jews believe in Jesus as their Messiah and have become part of the Church. In Ezekiel 34, God speaks at length about his people.

¹¹ For thus says the Lord God, "Behold, I Myself will search for My sheep and seek them out. ¹² As a shepherd cares for his herd in the day when he is among his scattered sheep, so I will care for My sheep and will deliver them from all the places to which they were scattered on a cloudy and gloomy day. ¹³ I will bring them out from the peoples and gather them from the countries and bring them to their own land; and I will feed them on the mountains of Israel, by the streams, and in all the inhabited places of the land. ¹⁴ I will feed them in a good pasture, and their grazing ground will be on the mountain heights of

Israel. There they will lie down on good grazing ground and feed in rich pasture on the mountains of Israel. ¹⁵ I will feed My flock and I will lead them to rest," declares the Lord God. ¹⁶ "I will seek the lost, bring back the scattered, bind up the broken and strengthen the sick; but the fat and the strong I will destroy. I will feed them with judgment.

¹⁷ "As for you, My flock, thus says the Lord God, 'Behold, I will judge between one sheep and another, between the rams and the male goats. ¹⁸ Is it too slight a thing for you that you should feed in the good pasture, that you must tread down with your feet the rest of your pastures? Or that you should drink of the clear waters, that you must foul the rest with your feet? ¹⁹ As for My flock, they must eat what you tread down with your feet and drink what you foul with your feet!'"

²⁰ Therefore, thus says the Lord God to them, "Behold, I, even I, will judge between the fat sheep and the lean sheep. ²¹ Because you push with side

and with shoulder, and thrust at all the weak with your horns until you have scattered them abroad, [22] therefore, I will deliver My flock, and they will no longer be a prey; and I will judge between one sheep and another.

[23] "Then I will set over them one shepherd, My servant David, and he will feed them; he will feed them himself and be their shepherd. [24] And I, the Lord, will be their God, and My servant David will be prince among them; I the Lord have spoken.

[25] "I will make a covenant of peace with them and eliminate harmful beasts from the land so that they may live securely in the wilderness and sleep in the woods. [26] I will make them and the places around My hill a blessing. And I will cause showers to come down in their season; they will be showers of blessing. [27] Also the tree of the field will yield its fruit and the earth will yield its increase, and they will be secure on their land. Then they will know that I am the Lord, when I have broken the

bars of their yoke and have delivered them from the hand of those who enslaved them. [28] They will no longer be a prey to the nations, and the beasts of the earth will not devour them; but they will live securely, and no one will make them afraid. [29] I will establish for them a renowned planting place, and they will not again be victims of famine in the land, and they will not endure the insults of the nations anymore. [30] Then they will know that I, the Lord their God, am with them, and that they, the house of Israel, are My people," declares the Lord God. [31] "As for you, My sheep, the sheep of My pasture, you are men, and I am your God," declares the Lord God (Ezekiel 34:11–31 New American Standard Bible 1995).

God's covenants with Israel will be fulfilled during the Millennial Kingdom when the Church Age ends and God's people are raptured out of this world and taken to be with the Lord. That will be followed by the Marriage Supper of the Lamb as the Bride of Christ, the Church, receives her heavenly reward. But until then, we the Church must press on through the Power of the Holy Spirit until that trumpet blast!

The Practice of Legalism. The term legalism is used by Christians to describe a doctrinal position emphasizing various rules and regulations pertaining to a person's Salvation and their spiritual growth. It comes down to a preoccupation of a person's form verses their actual spiritual growth as a follower of Jesus Christ.

Legalist may appear to be spiritual and righteous on the outside, but legalism always fails to achieve God's purposes because it is an outward performance rather than an inward healing and transformation into Christlikeness. It is a desire to appear holy before others. They are attempting to be justified before men rather than God.

[20] If you have died with Christ to the elementary principles of the world, why, as if you were living in the world, do you submit yourself to decrees, such as, [21] "Do not handle, do not taste, do not touch!" [22] (which all refer to things destined to perish with use)— in accordance with the commandments and teachings of men? [23] These are matters which have, to be sure, the appearance of wisdom in self-made religion and self-abasement and severe treatment of the body, but are of

no value against fleshly indulgence (Colossians 2:20–23 New American Standard Bible 1995).

Doctrinally speaking, legalists are essentially opposed to grace—an attitude that doesn't line up with Scripture. Heresy is a serious matter. It is when we adhere to a religious opinion that does not match that of Scripture. Any deviation from God's Word will be judged in a serious manner.

> [8] For by grace you have been saved through faith; and that not of yourselves, it is the gift of God; [9] not as a result of works, so that no one may boast (Ephesians 2:8–9 New American Standard Bible 1995).

> [9] who has saved us and called us with a holy calling, not according to our works, but according to His own purpose and grace which was granted us in Christ Jesus from all eternity (2 Timothy 1:9 New American Standard Bible 1995).

> [11] For the grace of God has appeared, bringing salvation to all men,
>
> [12] instructing us to deny ungodliness and worldly desires and to live sensibly,

righteously, and godly in the present age (Titus 2:11–12 New American Standard Bible 1995).

Legalism has been an issue ever since Satan deceived Eve into believing there was a better way of life for her compared to the one God created. Is anyone unbelieving of the fact that Satan is still up to all his lies and deceptions today? As I indicated before, Satan's main focus is to destroy anything or anyone associated to God in any way!

Legalism deceives churches and their members to part ways. Essentially, legalists demand a literal obedience to the law that *Christ fulfilled!* Jesus set the standard for all mankind to follow. He laid out the way we should live our lives by modeling it to us.

> [21] I do not nullify the grace of God, for if righteousness comes through the Law, then Christ died needlessly (Galatians 2:21 New American Standard Bible 1995).

Notice how Jesus responds to the Pharisees in Luke 11. He doesn't take part in their rituals, and they notice it immediately.

> [37] Now when He had spoken, a Pharisee asked Him to have lunch with him;

and He went in, and reclined at the table. ³⁸ When the Pharisee saw it, he was surprised that He had not first ceremonially washed before the meal. ³⁹ But the Lord said to him, "Now you Pharisees clean the outside of the cup and of the platter; but inside of you, you are full of robbery and wickedness. ⁴⁰ You foolish ones, did not He who made the outside make the inside also? ⁴¹ But give that which is within as charity, and then all things are clean for you.

⁴² "But woe to you Pharisees! For you pay tithe of mint and rue and every kind of garden herb, and yet disregard justice and the love of God; but these are the things you should have done without neglecting the others. ⁴³ Woe to you Pharisees! For you love the chief seats in the synagogues and the respectful greetings in the market places. ⁴⁴ Woe to you! For you are like concealed tombs, and the people who walk over them are unaware of it."

⁴⁵ One of the lawyers said to Him in reply, "Teacher, when You say this, You insult us too." ⁴⁶ But He said,

"Woe to you lawyers as well! For you weigh men down with burdens hard to bear, while you yourselves will not even touch the burdens with one of your fingers. [47] Woe to you! For you build the tombs of the prophets, and it was your fathers who killed them. [48] So you are witnesses and approve the deeds of your fathers; because it was they who killed them, and you build their tombs. [49] For this reason also the wisdom of God said, 'I will send to them prophets and apostles, and some of them they will kill and some they will persecute, [50] so that the blood of all the prophets, shed since the foundation of the world, may be charged against this generation, [51] from the blood of Abel to the blood of Zechariah, who was killed between the altar and the house of God; yes, I tell you, it shall be charged against this generation.' [52] Woe to you lawyers! For you have taken away the key of knowledge; you yourselves did not enter, and you hindered those who were entering." [53] When He left there, the scribes and the Pharisees began to be very hostile and to question Him closely on many subjects, [54] plotting against Him to catch Him in something He might say (Luke 11:37–54 New American Standard Bible).

Personal preferences can be a way we share our love toward others, but it is not right to demand others feel the same way. To avoid the trap of legalism, we must hold fast to God's Word—as evidence in Romans 14.

[10] But you, why do you judge your brother? Or you again, why do you regard your brother with contempt? For we will all stand before the judgment seat of God (Romans 14:10 New American Standard Bible 1995).

[4] Beloved, do not believe every spirit, but test the spirits to see whether they are from God, because many false prophets have gone out into the world (1 John 4:1 New American Standard Bible 1995).

Pandemics Now and Before. Perhaps you've pondered whether the coronavirus is a sign of the end times. Maybe you've wondered whether God Himself causes or allows pandemics and other diseases to occur. The Old Testament in particular describes various occasions when God brought plagues and diseases on Israel and His enemies. He used plagues on Egypt to force Pharaoh to free the Israelites from captivity, all while protecting His own people from becoming affected by them.

> [13] The blood shall be a sign for you on the houses where you live; and when I see the blood I will pass over you, and no plague will befall you to destroy you when I strike the land of Egypt (Exodus 12:13 New American Standard Bible 1995).

> [26] And He said, "If you will give earnest heed to the voice of the Lord your God, and do what is right in His sight, and give ear to His commandments, and keep all His statutes, I will put none of the diseases on you which I have put on the Egyptians; for I, the Lord, am your healer." (Exodus 15:26 New American Standard Bible 1995).

God also warned Israel of the consequences of their disobedience, which included plagues.

> [21] 'If then, you act with hostility against Me and are unwilling to obey Me, I will

increase the plague on you seven times according to your sins (Leviticus 26:21 New American Standard Bible 1995).

25 I will also bring upon you a sword which will execute vengeance for the covenant; and when you gather together into your cities, I will send pestilence among you, so that you shall be delivered into enemy hands (Leviticus 26:25 New American Standard Bible 1995).

When God reprimands us, it is always with the intention of repentance and restoration. We also have to realize we live in a sinful, fallen, and cursed world. So, we are going to experience various sicknesses, disease, and worldwide pandemics as a result. The bottom line is, God is Sovereign, and we are not!

39 'See now that I, I am He,
And there is no god besides Me;
It is I who put to death and give life.
I have wounded and it is I who heal,
And there is no one who can deliver from My hand (Deuteronomy 32:39 New American Standard Bible 1995).

The coronavirus is just a taste of things to come.

We are living in the last hours. If you haven't already, it's time to get right with the Lord. Jesus said:

> [11] and there will be great earthquakes, and in various places plagues and famines; and there will be terrors and great signs from heaven (Luke 21:11 New American Standard Bible 1995).

Life here on earth is fragile. Like I said before, we can be here one minute, and gone the next. And if you think this is bad, hell for all unbelievers will be far, far worse. So, repent today while you have an opportunity.

The Rapture of the Church. The Church Age will end with the Rapture of the Church. The Rapture, or the snatching away of the Church, is clearly taught in Scripture. God removes all believers from the earth before He pours out His righteous judgment during the Tribulation period.

> [51] Behold, I tell you a mystery; we will not all sleep, but we will all be changed, [52] in a moment, in the twinkling of an eye, at the last trumpet; for the trumpet will sound, and the dead will be raised imperishable, and we

will be changed. [53] For this perishable must put on the imperishable, and this mortal must put on immortality. [54] But when this perishable will have put on the imperishable, and this mortal will have put on immortality, then will come about the saying that is written, "Death is swallowed up in victory. [55] O death, where is your victory? O death, where is your sting?" [56] The sting of death is sin, and the power of sin is the law; [57] but thanks be to God, who gives us the victory through our Lord Jesus Christ (1 Corinthians 15:51–57 New American Standard Bible 1995).

Imagine your body being instantaneously transformed into a glorified body for all eternity. Christians everywhere will be miraculously changed in the twinkling of an eye. The Rapture of the Church should be at the forefront of all our minds. We should be fired up and excited to meet our Lord in the air! We will be in God's Holy Presence forever and ever! No more sin ever again. *We should all be rejoicing as we press on in these last hours.* Be intentional to encourage all our precious brothers and sisters in Christ every day that God so graciously gives us to live. Don't allow Satan to rob you of all this incredible joy and excitement!

> [2] Beloved, now we are children of God, and it has not appeared as yet what we will be. We know that when He appears, we will be like Him, because we will see Him just as He is (1 John 3:2 New American Standard Bible 1995).

The Rapture is the next event in God's prophetic timeline. There are no more prophecies that need to be fulfilled prior to the Rapture. It can happen literally at any moment. Do your beliefs match that of Scripture? This is not something to play around with! Humble yourself today.

The Unholy Trinity. What is frequently referred to as the "unholy trinity" is comprised of Satan, the Antichrist, and the False Prophet. They all play a prominent role in the book of Revelations. This cabal is the result of Satan's evil schemes; remember, Satan can't create like God can. He can only corrupt others that are willing to go along. Witchcraft is an expression of Satan's mimicry. Instead of God's miracles, the occult is offered as an alternative by the devil. There are people in all facets of life that are willing to go along to get along. It's part of our sinful nature. Satan is a counterfeit. He tries to emulate God and the Holy Trinity in an effort to deceive the human race. Don't believe his lies!

The Holy Trinity includes God the Father, Jesus Christ the Son, and the Holy Spirit. The Holy Trinity is characterized by unwavering truth, agape love, amazing grace and mercies, and infinite wisdom and power. On the other hand, the unholy trinity is a purely evil design meant to deceive the nations.

We need to realize we are no longer living in the Last Days. We are living in the Last Hours. Make sure you are being very watchful as Bible prophecy continues to unfold before our very eyes. The unholy trinity has banded together in an effort to thwart God's glorious plan from coming to fruition. They are also determined to prevent the unsaved from coming to know Jesus Christ as their Lord and Savior. They will also be specifically targeting Israel. Satan wants them to continue in their rebellion against God. In the end, of course, Satan and all his cohorts will lose miserably! I urge you today, don't be deceived anymore! Like I said before, get wise to how Satan operates, or you will regret it for all eternity!

Review the book of Revelations chapters twelve and thirteen. In it there are prophetic passages on the main figures and events to come. Satan will play a major role, yes, but God is ultimately in control. Chapter twelve expresses many different factors about Satan that should not be taken lightly! He intends evil toward all of us who know, love, and serve our Lord and Savior

Jesus Christ.

We would all agree our world has changed dramatically. Everything has been tipped upside down. Keep in mind, this is all part of the end times. We have to go through a season of this before we get to the other side. It's all part of the process leading to a complete renewal of Heaven and earth. Keep your heart and mind fixed on God and things above. Focus on spreading the Gospel and fulfilling your ministry for God's Glory and Honor! It's now or never.

The second member of the unholy trinity is the Antichrist, who is also known as the beast, described in Revelation chapter thirteen. He is indwelled by Satan. The Antichrist will form the final world kingdom, which will lead to a One World Government. It will be totally blasphemous toward the One True God who is ELOHIM.

The Antichrist will set himself up as God, and demand that the whole world worship him.

> [4] they worshiped the dragon because he gave his authority to the beast; and they worshiped the beast, saying, "Who is like the beast, and who is able to wage war with him?" [5] There was given to him a mouth speaking arrogant words and blasphemies, and authority

to act for forty-two months was given to him. [6] And he opened his mouth in blasphemies against God, to blaspheme His name and His tabernacle, that is, those who dwell in heaven.

[7] It was also given to him to make war with the saints and to overcome them, and authority over every tribe and people and tongue and nation was given to him (Revelation 13:4–7 New American Standard Bible 1995).

[3] Let no one in any way deceive you, for it will not come unless the apostasy comes first, and the man of lawlessness is revealed, the son of destruction, [4] who opposes and exalts himself above every so-called god or object of worship, so that he takes his seat in the temple of God, displaying himself as being God (2 Thessalonians 2:3–4).

[9] that is, the one whose coming is in accord with the activity of Satan, with all power and signs and false wonders, [10] and with all the deception of wickedness for those who perish, because they did not receive the love of the truth so as to be saved (2

Thessalonians New American Standard Bible 1995).

That is the abomination of desolation. The world will become completely enthralled by the Antichrist. At that point, he will become very emboldened, dispensing with all pretenses of being a peaceful ruler.

> [18] Children, it is the last hour; and just as you heard that antichrist is coming, even now many antichrists have appeared; from this we know that it is the last hour (1 John 2:18 New American Standard Bible 1995).

And what about Artificial Intelligence, which is quickly coming onto the scene? Imagine this technology in the hands of the unholy trinity and dictators around the world who want to eliminate us from the earth. It's time to quickly exclude any and all things in your life that are mere distractions from what is most important. That is your walk with God, your family, doing your homework, and fulfilling your ministry!

The third member of the unholy trinity is the False Prophet. Although he presents himself as a benevolent, meek, and mild person, he is not. Jesus warned Christians to watch out for false prophets that appear innocent but can be very destructive:

> [15] "Beware of the false prophets, who come to you in sheep's clothing, but inwardly are ravenous wolves (Matthew 7:15 New American Standard Bible 1995).

The False Prophet will speak persuasively and deceptively to turn humans away from God and encourage the worship of the Antichrist and Satan himself. The False Prophet will bring down fire from heaven including other signs and wonders. He will set up an image of the Antichrist and force everyone to worship him, and those who refuse, will be killed.

> [4] Then I saw thrones, and they sat on them, and judgment was given to them. And I saw the souls of those who had been beheaded because of their testimony of Jesus and because of the word of God, and those who had not worshiped the beast or his image, and had not received the mark on their forehead and on their hand; and they came to life and reigned with Christ for a thousand years (Revelation 20:4 New American Standard Bible 1995).

The False Prophet will then compel each person to receive a permanent mark of some type to show total devotion to the Antichrist and renunciation to God. And without the mark, you will not be able to buy or sell anything. And if you should decide to take the mark, the Bible makes it very clear that you're not only accepting an economic system, but also a worship system that excludes Jesus Christ. *This couldn't be more serious!*

> [18] Here is wisdom. Let him who has understanding calculate the number of the beast, for the number is that of a man; and his number is six hundred and sixty-six (Revelation 13:18 New American Standard Bible 1995).

Dear brothers and sisters in Christ, God's Kingdom will prevail. Don't ever doubt it. Get prayed up, we're going up!

> [21] I kept looking, and that horn was waging war with the saints and overpowering them [22] until the Ancient of Days came and judgment was passed in favor of the saints of the Highest One, and the time arrived when the saints took possession of the kingdom (Daniel 7:21–22 New American Standard Bible

1995).

One World Religion. The One World Religion that will be part of the end-times scenario is also known as the great harlot, found in the book of Revelation chapter 17, verses 1–18. The term harlot is used as a metaphor for those who follow false religions which will be given full authority by the Antichrist. The harlot will commit adultery with the kings of the earth, referring to false religions influencing world leaders and influential people who get drunk on the power they receive from worshiping a false god from a false religion, which are all devoid of the soul-saving gospel. Because of their lust for power, it drives them away from the One True Living God. This will enable them to dominate all people from all nations around the world.

Jesus warns us below that the deception will be so great, that if it were possible, even the elect would be deceived. The days of just going through the motions as a Christian are over!

> [24] For false Christs and false prophets will arise and will show great signs and wonders, so as to mislead, if possible, even the elect (Matthew 24:24 New American Standard Bible 1995).

One World Government. The One World

Government will be blasphemous, denying the One True God! The Antichrist who was given his power from the devil will wage war on God's holy people and conquer them. Then the Antichrist will be recognized as sovereign leader of the world. There are some governments today that are willing to give up some of their sovereignty to combat climate change, for example. Imagine all the disasters and plagues yet to come. It will be so monumental that the nations around the world will gladly welcome anyone or anything that offers a solution to all their problems.

At that point Satan will move to establish total control of all the world. He will demand that mankind worship him which will edge him closer to his greatest desire, and that is to be like God. To control people, you must first control commerce. All those who are left behind after the Rapture of the Church will face an excruciating decision. Either accept the mark of the beast, or face starvation and horrible persecution from the Antichrist and all his followers.

The Tribulation. The Rapture of the Church will be followed by the Tribulation. The Tribulation is a seven-year period that will begin when the Antichrist signs a peace covenant with Israel. And it will end with the Second Coming of Jesus Christ. This will be the final seven years of earth's history. Just incredible!

There are two main purposes for the

Tribulation. The first is a time for Salvation for both Jews and Gentiles. Many people will be saved during this time. This is another example of God's Amazing Grace and Mercy toward mankind. The second purpose will be a time of great condemnation toward unbelievers who have rejected Christ's death on the Cross.

> [9] The Lord is not slow about His promise, as some count slowness, but is patient toward you, not wishing for any to perish but for all to come to repentance (2 Peter 3:9 New American Standard Bible 1995).

> [9] If we confess our sins, He is faithful and righteous to forgive us our sins and to cleanse us from all unrighteousness (1 John 1:9 New American Standard Bible 1995).

> [12] "Now at that time Michael, the great prince who stands guard over the sons of your people, will arise. And there will be a time of distress such as never occurred since there was a nation until that time; and at that time your people, everyone who is found written in the book, will be rescued (Daniel 12:1 New American Standard Bible 1995).

> [7] 'Alas! for that day is great, there is none like it;
> And it is the time of Jacob's distress, but he will be saved from it (Jeremiah 30:7 New American Standard Bible).

The phrase "Jacob's distress" is referring to the nation of Israel. Which will experience persecution and natural disasters that have never been seen or experienced before in all of history. Pray for precious Israel every day, that they all would come into the Kingdom of God through the Cross of Christ Jesus our Lord and Savior, amen!

Armageddon and the Second Coming of Christ. The Bible refers to Armageddon as a climactic future battle between God and all the forces of evil described in the book of Revelation. Demonic influences will cause the kings of the earth to gather their armies for an all-out assault against Jerusalem. The Antichrist will be leading the charge. This will be the final world conflict.

> [13] And I saw coming out of the mouth of the dragon and out of the mouth of the beast and out of the mouth of the false prophet, three unclean spirits like frogs; [14] for they are spirits of demons, performing signs, which go out to the kings of the whole world, to gather

them together for the war of the great day of God, the Almighty. [15] ("Behold, I am coming like a thief. Blessed is the one who stays awake and keeps his clothes, so that he will not walk about naked and men will not see his shame.") [16] And they gathered them together to the place which in Hebrew is called Har-Magedon (Revelation 16:13–16 New American Standard Bible 1995).

[3] And I will bless those who bless you,
And the one who curses you I will curse.
And in you all the families of the earth will be blessed." (Genesis 12:3 New American Standard Bible 1995).

Jesus Christ will return to earth with the armies of Heaven by His side. His feet will stand on the Mount of Olives. He will defeat all the forces of evil.

[15] From His mouth comes a sharp sword, so that with it He may strike down the nations, and He will rule them with a rod of iron; and He treads the wine press of the fierce wrath of God, the Almighty. [16] And on His robe and on His thigh He has a name

written, "KING OF KINGS, AND LORD OF LORDS." (Revelation 19:15–16 New American Standard Bible 1995).

He will cast the Antichrist and the false prophet into the lake of fire.

> [20] And the beast was seized, and with him the false prophet who performed the signs in his presence, by which he deceived those who had received the mark of the beast and those who worshiped his image; these two were thrown alive into the lake of fire which burns with brimstone (Revelation 19:20 New American Standard Bible 1995).

Then He will bind Satan, and set up His Kingdom for one thousand years, and all things will be made right. Praise God every day for what He has done, for what He is doing, and for what He is about to do very soon!

The Millennium. The Millennium, which is also known as the Millennium Kingdom, is a thousand-year period when Christ will reign on the earth. This occurs after the Tribulation, and before the Great White Throne Judgment. During this time frame, Jesus will rule over Israel and all the nations of the world. We will all live in peace.

Can you imagine? Praise God Almighty!

> [4] And He will judge between the nations,
> And will render decisions for many peoples;
> And they will hammer their swords into plowshares,
> and their spears into pruning hooks.
> Nation will not lift up sword against nation,
> And never again will they learn war (Isaiah 2:4 New American Standard Bible 1995).

> [1] "Behold, My Servant, whom I uphold;
> My chosen one in whom My soul delights.
> I have put My Spirit upon Him;
> He will bring forth justice to the nations (Isaiah 42:1 New American Standard Bible 1995).

The purpose of the thousand-year reign is to fulfill various promises that God made to the world. Some of these promises known as covenants, were given to Israel. There were also some given to Jesus, the nations around the world, and creation. God promised the curse would be lifted. All animals on the earth would be restored. Human beings would be freed from disease. This is another example of God keeping all His promises. We just have to remember; it's all in His perfect timing and not ours. Have faith, will travel.

> [18] For I consider that the sufferings of this present time are not worthy to be compared with the glory that is to be revealed to us. [19] For the anxious longing of the creation waits eagerly for the revealing of the sons of God. [20] For the creation was subjected to futility, not willingly, but because of Him who subjected it, in hope [21] that the creation itself also will be set free from its slavery to corruption into the freedom of the glory of the children of God. [22] For we know that the whole creation groans and suffers the pains of childbirth together until now. [23] And not only this, but also we ourselves, having the first fruits of the Spirit, even we ourselves groan within ourselves, waiting eagerly for our adoption as sons, the redemption of our body (Romans 8:18–23 New American Standard Bible 1995).

The only thing Satan could ever promise

mankind is death and destruction. Satan and all those who follow him are doomed to hell forever. This should greatly encourage us all to take God at His word. Press on dear brothers and sisters in Christ!

Satan Released and the Final Rebellion. Satan has always been the enemy of mankind. Satan hates us with a special kind of hatred. Ever since Satan's fall, he has been the adversary of Israel and Christians.

> [44] You are of your father the devil, and you want to do the desires of your father. He was a murderer from the beginning, and does not stand in the truth because there is no truth in him. Whenever he speaks a lie, he speaks from his own nature, for he is a liar and the father of lies (John 8:44 New American Standard Bible 1995).

> [22] Who is the liar but the one who denies that Jesus is the Christ? This is the antichrist, the one who denies the Father and the Son (1 John 2:22 New American Standard Bible 1995).

At the end of the Millennial Reign of Jesus Christ, Satan will be released for a short time. You might be wondering, why would God release Satan?

Only believers enter the Millennium. We do so in our new glorified bodies that we received from God at the Rapture. Our glorified bodies are not designed to reproduce, but natural bodies are. Therefore, people who become born-again and were not killed during the Tribulation Period, will enter the Millennium in their natural bodies. That means they will be able to have children.

It is necessary that every single person be given the choice to become a follower of Christ or not. Because of that, God will free Satan for a short time. And amazingly, some children who were born and raised during the Millennium will choose Satan over Christ. That is known as the final rebellion.

> [7] When the thousand years are completed, Satan will be released from his prison, [8] and will come out to deceive the nations which are in the four corners of the earth, Gog and Magog, to gather them together for the war; the number of them is like the sand of the seashore. [9] And they came up on the broad plain of the earth and surrounded the camp of the saints and the beloved city, and fire came down from heaven and devoured them. [10] And the devil who deceived

them was thrown into the lake of fire and brimstone, where the beast and the false prophet are also; and they will be tormented day and night forever and ever (Revelation 20:7–10 New American Standard Bible 1995).

At the end of the thousand years, God will have zero tolerance for any form of sin and rebellion. When it happens, He will show no mercy and offer no second chances. At that time, God will be quick to judge. The final rebellion from Satan and sinful man will be over in a heartbeat. Eternity will begin with all sin gone for all time. Where do you stand today?

The Great White Throne Judgement. The second judgment will be that of unbelievers. This judgment does not determine a person's salvation. It has already been determined. Everyone at the Great White Throne Judgment is an unbeliever. They have rejected Christ in this life, and therefore are doomed to the lake of fire.

5 But because of your stubbornness and unrepentant heart you are storing up wrath for yourself in the day of wrath and revelation of the righteous judgment of God, (Romans 2:5 New American Standard Bible 1995).

No amount of "good works" and the keeping of God's laws can be sufficient to atone for sin. All their thoughts, words, and deeds will be judged against God's perfect Holy and Righteous standard. All those who have rejected Jesus Christ as their Lord and Savior will regret it for all eternity! There will be no reward for them. Only eternal condemnation and punishment. Can you imagine?

> [11] Then I saw a great white throne and Him who sat upon it, from whose presence earth and heaven fled away,
>
> and no place was found for them. [12] And I saw the dead, the great and the small, standing before the throne, and books were opened; and another book was opened, which is the book of life; and the dead were judged from the things which were written in the books,
>
> according to their deeds. [13] And the sea gave up the dead which were in it, and death and Hades gave up the dead which were in them; and they were judged, every one of them according to their deeds. [14] Then death and Hades were thrown into the lake of fire. This is the second death, the lake of fire. [15] And if

anyone's name was not found written in the book of life, he was thrown into the lake of fire (Revelation 20:11–15 New American Standard Bible 1995).

[16] Nevertheless knowing that a man is not justified by the works of the Law but through faith in Christ Jesus, even we have believed in Christ Jesus, so that we may be justified by faith in Christ and not by the works of the Law; since by the works of the Law no flesh will be justified (Galatians 2:16 New American Standard Bible 1995).

In order for a person to get right with God, we must first understand what is wrong. The problem is sin. The bad news is the penalty for sin is death. You hear unbelievers say, I don't need Jesus Christ's forgiveness. I'm good enough to get to heaven on my own. The problem for unbelievers is, the standard by which God judges is the perfection of Jesus Christ. That's why the world hates Jesus.

[3] They have all turned aside, together they have become corrupt; there is no one who does good, not even one (Psalm 14:3 New American Standard Bible 1995).

Keep in mind, unbelievers are not destroyed when they are judged. They will suffer forever and ever. The truth about hell is the fact that after you have spent a trillion years in the agony of hell, you will not have reduced your time there by one second. That is the fate of everyone who dies and has rejected Christ's death on the Cross for the penalty of their sins.

Eternity Everlasting. Heaven is the dwelling place of God. The invisible realm of God Almighty. Our eternal abode, however, is the new earth which will come with a new Heaven and is referred to as the eternal state. The old heaven and earth will be destroyed.

> [10] But the day of the Lord will come like a thief, in which the heavens will pass away with a roar and the elements will be destroyed with intense heat, and the earth and its works will be burned up.
>
> [11] Since all these things are to be destroyed in this way, what sort of people ought you to be in holy conduct and godliness, [12] looking for and hastening the coming of the day of God, because of which the heavens will be destroyed by burning, and the elements will melt with intense heat! [13]

But according to His promise we are looking for new heavens and a new earth, in which righteousness dwells (2 Peter 3:10–13 New American Standard Bible 1995).

The eternal state is the final piece in God's plan, where the earth will be restored to its original design, accompanied with the New Heaven. Have we, the Bride of Christ, made ourselves ready for His return?

[1] Then he showed me a river of the water of life, clear as crystal, coming from the throne of God and of the Lamb, [2] in the middle of its street. On either side of the river was the tree of life, bearing twelve kinds of fruit, yielding its fruit every month; and the leaves of the tree were for the healing of the nations. [3] There will no longer be any curse; and the throne of God and of the Lamb will be in it, and His bond-servants will serve Him; [4] they will see His face, and His name will be on their foreheads (Revelation 22:1–4 New American Standard Bible 1995).

Believers will have access to the Holy City, the

New Jerusalem, and the Tree of Life. *Get ready to rejoice like never before!*

> [4] And He will wipe away every tear from their eyes; and there will no longer be any death; there will no longer be any mourning, or crying, or pain; the first things have passed away." (Revelation 21:4 New American Standard Bible 1995).

This is not our home! The trumpet is soon to blast, and the clouds will part, and we will see with our own eyes, the King of Kings, and the Lord of Lords. Absolutely incredible! Heaven is not going to be boring like some people think! That is another lie from Satan.

In Heaven, we will no longer be under the curse of sin. We will never again be motivated by anything other than our love for God. Everything we do will be untainted by our old sin nature. There will be no secrets in Heaven. We won't have to be ashamed of anything anymore. You will have nothing to hide. Heaven will be a place of infinite learning.

> [34] "Then the King will say to those on His right, 'Come, you who are blessed of My Father, inherit the kingdom prepared for you from the foundation

of the world (Matthew 25:34 New American Standard Bible 1995).

What all we will be doing in Heaven, we can be well assured it will be most wonderful, far beyond our wildest imaginations. To God be the Glory, Amen!

Jesus told us to store up for ourselves treasures in Heaven. He directly linked this command to the desires of our heart.

> [20] But store up for yourselves treasures in heaven, where neither moth nor rust destroys, and where thieves do not break in or steal; [21] for where your treasure is, there your heart will be also (Matthew 6:20–21 New American Standard Bible 1995).

Have you humbly searched your heart lately? If you haven't, it's time to do so! Eternity has no beginning and no end!

Dear Heavenly Father, as Your children, we want to thank You for dying on the Cross to pay the penalty for our sins! Had You not done that, we would all be headed straight to hell. Our lives are yours to do with as you please. We love You and praise You always and forever! We also pray for each person reading this book. We ask that the eyes of their hearts would be opened. We pray that they would repent of their sins and place their faith in Christ's death alone for the forgiveness of their sins, and believe that You raised Him from the dead, so that they may be saved. We pray too for every precious brother and sister in Christ. That wherever they are in their walk with you, Lord, that they would keep growing in their faith. That they would press on through any difficulty. That they would keep their hearts and minds fixed on You and on the things above. That they would fulfill their precious ministry for Your Glory and Honor. We humbly pray too, Lord, for the forgiveness of our sins in the body of Christ at large. And we pray for wisdom to reject the lies and deceptions of Satan's evil schemes in this sinful, fallen, and cursed world in which we live. And we pray, Lord, for everyone to turn back to Your Holy and precious Word. *In Jesus' name we pray, Amen!*

References

Missler, N. (2009). The way of agape: Understanding God's love [DVD]. King's High Way.

The Lockman Foundation. (1995). *The New American Standard Bible* (NASB). Lockman Foundation.

Yerkovich, M., & Yerkovich, K. (2009). *How we love*. WaterBrook.

About the Author

I have been married to my precious wife Michelle for twenty-seven years. I was nearly twenty-five years old when I was involved in a motorcycle accident and given a one percent chance to live. Against all odds, I survived and have been a C5 quadriplegic for the past thirty-five years. Eighteen months into my injury I became a Christian when my nurse shared the Gospel with me. Over the years I attended the School of Hard Knocks, which taught me many important lessons about life that I love to share with others. Today I am completely focused on fulfilling my ministry as a Christian and as a husband—all for God's Glory! Praise His Holy name!

Visit www.lynm.org for more of my books to come, and my blog. I also have a selection of practical Bible verses named *What Would Jesus Do?* —perfect for spur-of-the-moment mediations on God's Word.

Made in the USA
Monee, IL
12 July 2024

61444260R00197